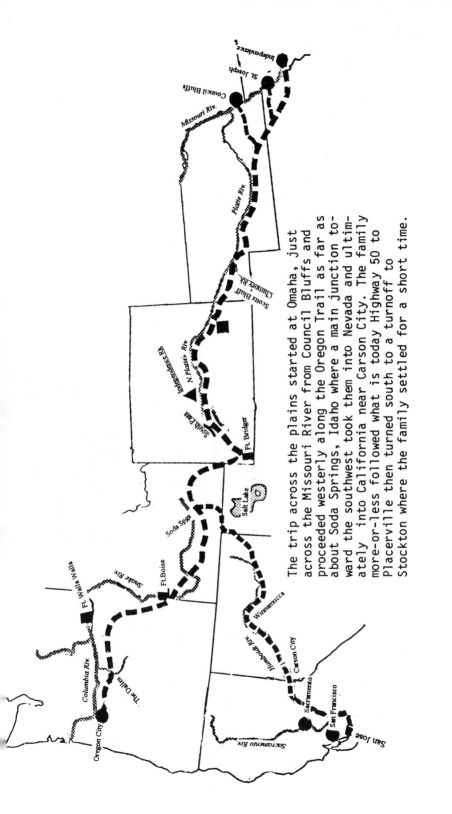

The trip across the plains started at Omaha, just across the Missouri River from Council Bluffs and proceeded westerly along the Oregon Trail as far as about Soda Springs, Idaho where a main junction toward the southwest took them into Nevada and ultimately into California near Carson City. The family more-or-less followed what is today Highway 50 to Placerville then turned south to a turnoff to Stockton where the family settled for a short time.

The Gould family before leaving for California.
George Albert, Albert H., Frank Horace, Jane Augusta
Gould. (lower) Albert H. Gould died in February 1863
just four months after arriving in California. In
June 1864, Jane married Levi Tourtillott then reared
five more children. These were (front row) Howard
Holbrook, Jane Augusta, Walter Wallace. (Back row),
True Trevor, Millie Augusta, Ernest Levi.

Diary of Jane Gould

"...after a fifteen mile drive without water or feed arrived
within sight of Humboldt City. Here we have no grass. The
cattle just have to browse...."

Photograph made August 1986 in the Forty Mile Desert of
Nevada during a field trip there during the annual convention
of the Oregon-California Trails Association.

Photo by Bert Webber

THE OREGON & CALIFORNIA TRAIL
DIARY OF
JANE GOULD IN 1862
Illustrated with Pictures, Map

**The Unabridged Diary
with Introduction and
Contemporary Comments by
BERT WEBBER**

WEBB RESEARCH GROUP PUBLISHERS

Please direct all inquiries to the Publisher:

WEBB RESEARCH GROUP PUBLISHERS
Books About the Oregon Country
P. O. Box 314
Medford, Oregon 97501 U.S.A.

Cover photograph by Bert Webber

An antique covered weapon displayed at Sunny Valley, Oregon in summer 1996. The site is on Interstate-5 a few miles north of Grants Pass at the Sunny Valley - Leland exit.

Leland, and Grave Creek, nearby, are identified by the Grave Creek Covered Bridge just off the east side of the freeway. This site is on the Applegate Trail, the southern route into Oregon from Idaho. For details, see the new book *Over the Applegate Trail to Oregon in 1846* by Bert Webber.

Library of Congress Cataloging-in-Publication Data:

Gould, Jane A. b. 1833 - 1917
    The Oregon & California trail diary of Jane Gould in 1862.
    Bibliography: p. 90
    Includes Index.
    1. Gould, Jane, 1833-1917–Diaries. 2. Overland journeys to the Pacific. 3. Pioneers–West (U.S.)–Diaries. 4. West (U.S.I–Description and travel–1860-1880. 5. California Trail. 6. Oregon Trail. I. Webber, Bert. II. Title. III. Title: The Oregon and California Trail Diary of Jane Gold in 1862.
[F594.G687]   917.8'042   87-14249
ISBN 0-936738-22-7

TABLE OF CONTENTS

Bert Webber is a Research Photojournalist. He writes books about what he calls, "the fantastic Pacific Northwest and the overland migration that helped build it." He is listed in *Who's Who in the West* and in *Contemporary Authors*. For a list of his many books see "Author's Index" of *Books in Print* in libraries and in book stores.

Some members of the Oregon-California Trails
Association (see page 92), on a field trip
in summer 1986 in the desert crossed by Jane
Gould 123 years earlier. Some traces of wagon
ruts remain. Area not far from Fallon, Nevada.
Photo by Bert Webber

INTRODUCTION

Albert and Jane Gould were apparently from Iowa. At least their trip across the plains starts in the center of that state with the first place name easily locatable today being Bradford in Franklin County, a village about 45 miles northwest of Waterloo. Other early place locations mentioned include Hardin County and Marshall County which shows their first direction was generally south. They mention having passed through Nevada in Storey County which indicates they were now on a Westward track but they jogged south again when they camped "just west of Des Moines." From here, following a contemporary road atlas, one can trace their route southwesterly to Council Bluffs. After crossing the Missouri River, they went to Omaha where they had a two week layover before hitting the trail.

A very common term throughout this diary has to do with "nooning." Or, "we nooned...." This was the term for the lunch or dinner break but far more was done during the "nooning" than merely eating and taking a snooze. This was the major daylight-hours break. A time when routine maintenance on the wagon was done, horses, mules, oxen shod, and if conditions were right, the women did the baking. Often, as we shall discover, the end-of-day's camp was not set up until after dark and often a day's march started well before sunup. Thus, the "nooning" was the single most important time of the 24-hour day to get things done other than actual travel.

Regretably, we know almost nothing about these folks. There is nothing in the diary to shed light on why they decided to make the trip. We do not know Albert's age. Jane Augusta (Holbrook) Gould was born in 1833 but we are not informed where. Her wedding date is not disclosed, but at age 20, her first son, George Albert, was born. The second son, Frank Horace came in 1855. They left on the cross-country trek when she was 29. We don't know anything about the state of their health but Jane was obviously the more durable for Albert is often ill and forced to take to the bed. There are no indications as to the nature of his ailment. Although this family successfully made the trip to Stockton, California, Albert died about one year later—cause not given.

Two other principals are continually mentioned throughout the work. "Lou," as Jane often identifies her is Lucy (Gould) Wyman, Albert's sister. The two women are fond of each other and plausibly their being together on this ardous trip allowed each to have someone close to talk with and let off frustrations of the trip of which there were many. We have no indication whether Albert or Lucy was the older.

The "Charley" often mentioned, was Lucy's husband. They had no children. We have no indication of what became of Charles and Lucy after Albert died. For remarks concerning Jane's further adventures, see the Epilogue.

Some writers of overland journals provide an introductory sketch or the truth of why pioneers left home for the "foreign" west—emigrants—comes through in the various diary entries. But not here. This diarist, Jane Gould, simply starts writing the day the family left. That she had some education is evident as will be noted by her usage and structure of the language. She was seldom curt. Yet there are unknowns about her diary. For this work, a transcript we had access to undoubtedly took some liberties with the original.

How much is unknown. The lack of good punctuation in the transcript could have been Jane's, or that of the transcriber. This writer was able to briefly scan a photostat of the diary but that copy had been badly handled and many pages are unclear. We were told the original was burned in a house fire.

Jane follows a format listing the day then the date. She makes a statement having to do with time of day for getting underway. She may not give exact clock time, but one gets the idea of time by her choice of words.

Jane Gould could be counted on as a weather observer and she often describes the location and condition of their camp sites. There is little hint of religion as her Sunday entries vary little from her writings for any other day of the week. If the family did not travel on Sunday those days seem to have been taken up with chores like doing the family wash or baking, etc. There does not seem to be any observance of Sunday as the Sabbath with one notable exception when Jane mentions there was a preaching service that she attended. There is no indication that anyone other than herself went with her. Sunday's were often used as rest days but this seems primarily to rest the animals.

The diary is matter-of-fact yet never reads like a chore although each day's activity was a near carbon copy of the earlier, but events creep in to provide excellent reader excitment. Nevertheless, the trip was a long, hard trudge. She gets homesick and twice wanted to quit. And, oh, how she hated the constant dust! There must have been dust in everything! The dust seemed more threatening to her than her homesickness or even hostile Indians. Their party would skirt some of those. On one occasion she wrote, "The dust is even worse than Indians, storms, or winds, or mosquitoes, or even wood ticks!" In another entry she indicates great vexation how she would give just about anything if she could just get a bath! But as pointed out, Jane had a buddy, sister-in-law Lucy. Good old Lou! Together they must have shared a lot of stress and obviously shared each others challenges and concerns. Although some might think it a play on words, no where in the diary did we discover Jane ever used the word "problem" when describing a situation.

Many who started on the Oregon Trail had specific destinations in mind. Some were pretty general, "Just want to get a farm in Oregon," or "going for gold" during the rush of the 49ers. Some were going to join family or friends who had made the trip in earlier years. Still others, even at this late date in overland travel had no destination and would decide once on the road based on circumstances. This latter seems to have been the venture of the Goulds—no destination.

Incidentally, about the names of various trails, and Jane remarks about these now and then, there are a lot of different names given to trails. In the early days what has now come to be known as the Oregon Trail was just called the Old Emigrant Trail. But the route, at least through Nebraska and most of Wyoming was, as Merrill J. Mattes titles his book, *The Great Platte River Road*. Just about everybody took it along one side or the other or the Platte River, then at the forks, the North Platte. The Applegate Trail was a southern approach to the Willamette Valley of Oregon which would miss the Blue Mountains and the long "float" down the Columbia River then portage around the falls in that river. The California Trail took off from the Applegate Trail to Carson City then over the Sierra Nevada Mountains. Common among various shortcuts are the Sublette Cutoff and the Lander Road. Jane had a guidebook but she does not identify the book until the mention of "Fremont" (page 43) which it undoubtedly was.

In some books, the perils of being stuck on the trail with a broken wagon or other personal disaster

s seemingly puffed out of proportion to any real
anger. But each year brought different circum-
tances yet a pattern became evident as more and more
eople went west. Early on there were few Indian
oncerns but in the early days of the movement there
ere not so many trains. Cholera seems to have been
 later hazzard but scurvey was always a risk. True,
here was nothing pleasant about having a breakdown
ut by the time, 1862, when the Goulds were on the
rail there were so many westward-bound wagons that
ad one been able to view the scene from today's jet
irliners at 38,000 feet altitude, the migrants would
ook to be almost a solid line. Many trains were less
han a mile apart. If there was trouble, the folks in
he following train, maybe 30 minutes away, could and
ften would render assistance.

For whatever reason the Gould's found themselves
n a certain "order" of march on Sunday, August 10,
hen a train about six miles ahead of them was
ttacked by Indians. She tells how word was passed
rom one train to another all the way back to their
osition and how men scrambled for their weapons to
nswer the alert. Jane Gould tells what she could
earn of the attack and massacre in good detail
tarting with her entry for that date. Then she
ontinues with the subject for the next several days.
er account is a good one. The location is easily
found today along the Interstate freeway a few miles
vest of the city of American Falls in Idaho. An area
has been set aside and is now called Massacre Rocks
State Park.

Recalling we are working from a transcript, we have
left what we presume to be close to Jane's original
wording pretty much alone. But we did modernize and
standardize some spellings. As examples: Jane used
"k" for the word "canyon." When they stayed overnight,
it was "staid." We also did away with a plethora of
commas present which could have been her way of
punctuation, or plausibly typos by the transcriber.

For clarity and for update notes as to locations, where I had added something these additions are set in [brackets]. Our object is to publish a readable account of this great adventure for new generations to enjoy.

For instance in this project the editor is indebted to many, but colleague Richard Portal, Master Reference Librarian, retired, of Salem, Oregon searched for details about the Gould family. We discovered traces during the 1920's in Coquille and in Alleganey both in Coos County, Oregon but these threads by now seem to have disappeared. It seemed plausible some Goulds' might turn up in the area between Stockton and Santa Clara in California, but searches there proved fruitless. Likewise, under Jane Gould's second husband's name, Levi Tourtillott, our inquiries in the San Joaquin Valley and in San Francisco were unrewarding.

We are also indebted to several folks in the Idaho State Historical Association for their searching and assistance on this project, as well as for help by personnel at Massacre Rocks State Park. We appreciate the special interest and willing assistance from Rick Just, Information Chief in Idaho State Parks and Recreation Commission.

We thank Karen Bolz Cramer, whose ancestors came west over the trail, for her close attention to our present typing and for her constant seeking additional clarifications as she worked with the material. And to my wife, Margie, a Registered Nurse, who spent several years in Public Health, for insight into "woman's ways" especially concerning matters of health along the way, as well as for her keen ear for listening as I read parts of the diary to her.

Bert Webber
Central Point, Oregon   March 1987

THE DIARY

1862

Sunday, April 27. Left home this morning, traveled through sloughy prairie, found some hay in an old stack, nooned, and went on to camp four miles from Chickisaw, camped in a grove near a house where we got grain and hay for our teams. The lady of the house offered us some milk but we had that. Came sixteen miles.

Monday, April 28. Arose early this morning. Gus went on before us [but] when we came to a [railroad] train [overpass] he had to fasten the oxen to the back of the wagon and pull us back as the cover would not go [under the track]. Passed through Chickisaw and Bradford, traveled 16 miles, camped at a small place called Norton, had a very pretty camping place.

Tuesday, April 29. When we got up this morning found a white frost on everything. The weather is rather cool for camping yet. Having no stove it is rather unpleasant cooking. Our road is very good today. We traveled 20 miles, came through Waverly which is on the Red Cedar. It is quite a brisk little place, also came through Shellrock City which is a pretty little town with a splendid water power. Camped in a grove.

Wednesday, April 30. It was raining this morning when we awoke. Had to get breakfast in the rain, having no tent. Came three miles, stopped at Willoughby to get the horses shod. It is a small prairie town in Butler County. We also passed through New Hartford, a little town on Beaver Creek. We came several miles on the Beaver bottoms, a low, swampy country. Stayed all night on the bank of the same stream. Could get no hay for the teams. Rained hard nearly all night. Rained through the [wagon] cover so we were wet some in the morning. Made 15 miles today.

Thursday, May 1. Took nearly an hour to build a fire this morning the ground was very wet and the wind blew cold from the northwest. Started late, bought some hay during the forenoon, carried it in bundles, nooned in a grove, camped for night near an old house which served as a wind breaker. We were right across the way from Fountain Post Office. Had to go back a mile for hay. Traveled 23 miles.

Friday, May 2. Left camp quite early, nooned in the edge of the timber, passed through Eldora a little prairie town in Hardin County. Had to carry hay 3 miles. Camped on the South Fork of the Iowa. Didn't get to camp till sundown. Made biscuits and baked them in the house near where we stopped. We learned we were one day behind the Mitchell Californians. Some boys came with some eggs to sell. We bought some of them. Came 23 miles.

Saturday, May 3. Traveled most of the time in Marshall County. Nooned in a grove in an Irish settlement. In the afternoon passed an old camping ground on Minerva Creek where we camped two years ago. We started at two o'clock across a twelve mile prairie not knowing it was so far and kept going and going until it came dark. Finally came to a house about nine o'clock but the man could let us have no hay so there was nothing to do but go on a mile farther. We made a fire and boiled some coffee. Bought some bread. Were just eating when Gus came up with the ox team. The men did not get to bed till twelve. We had company in camping. Two men going to Pikes Peak.

Sunday, May 4. After being so late we did not feel like hurrying. The Pike Peakers brought over a pail full of new milk for us. Came over a six mile prairie to Nevada, a prairie town the county seat of Story County. Came through a slough threefourths of a mile across. The mud was knee deep to the horses and not a resting spell. It was Skunk river bottom. We crossed the river to a little town, Cambridge, could get no hay so we came out of town a mile and camped in the prairie.

Monday, May 5. Started early this morning. Came over a very good country mostly prairie and nooned in a grove near a creek. Found the Mitchell Californians a goodly company of seven wagons. Stopped for the night just west of Des Moines. Came through the town, a nice flourishing town the capital of Iowa. The state house is of brick. There is an excellent bridge over the Des Moines River.

Tuesday, May 6. Started at Ten o'clock, traveled thirteen miles. Camped on Sugar Creek with a family moving from Des Moines.

Wednesday, May 7. Left Sugar Creek early. Came ten miles and ferried Coon River at a town named Abel, the county town of Dallas County. Came 19 miles. Camped near a town on a little creek.

Thursday, May 8. It was late when we left our camp. Came nine miles and camped to wash and wait for the other teams. I began washing at four and did a real large wash. Got it spread out to dry by sunset and was tired enough to go to bed. We stayed in a woolen factory.

Friday, May 9. The other teams came up. We went to the ferry but most of the company preferred to ford at a very steep ford, and did. We among the rest. Nooned on the prairie. Camped at six o'clock on the prairie a mile west of Dalmanutha, a prairie burgh in Guthrie County. The timber in this part of the country is very sparse. The prairie is rolling. We have excellent roads. Traveled 20 miles.

Saturday, May 10. Left our camp soon after sunrise. Came sixteen miles over good roads. Nooned in the road in front of a tavern. Boiled some eggs on the stove of one of our neighbors. Traveled most of the afternoon on the Turkey River bottom. It is beautiful land; the prairies look quite green. Camped near a little creek. The boys brought in some plum blossoms [which] were very refreshing.

Sunday, May 11. Started rather late this morning. Had a very pleasant forenoon. Came through a small town by the name of Grove City; saw there a wildcat in a cage. They feed it on chickens and meat. He looked real angry, would paw at a stick when the children put one through the bars. We crossed the Turkey. On its banks were near a dozen wagons laying over for the Sabbath (the women were washing). We came a mile and a half and camped at Lewis, the county town of Cass County. It is a small town on the prairie. We stopped at noon to wait until Monday. It is showery. Most all of the families are cooking beans today. Rained hard all night.

Monday, May 12. The rain had ceased when we arose. The sky was clear with a northwest wind. Traveled over a rolling prairie, nooned on a small prairie creek, came on a ridge road all of the afternoon. We were without water and almost suffered for the want of it. At last came to a house where we found some real good water. Camped at night on the bank of a small creek. We bought some wood. There were some thirty wagons of all. Had some fiddling in the evening in one of the tents.

Tuesday, May 13. We left our encampment on the creek at seven this morning. Have passed through some very pretty country, a beautiful grove and crossed the West Nishnabotna [River] where there was a grist mill. Met some pretty little girls going to school. Stopped for noon early at 10 o'clock on account of the heat. Went off the road half a mile to camp on account of there being no feed on the road. Found a spring which by digging out yielded very good water. The country over which we came today has been rather rough but good land.

Wednesday, May 14. The weather was warm and fair this morning. Had a fine road, nooned near a little prairie creek. Near its banks we found a spring of nice cool water. After going some ten miles we came to the Missouri River bottom which is very bad. After five miles of this road we came to Council Bluffs, a real lively town in this season of the year when there are so many fitting out for the trip to and beyond the Rocky Mountains. We camped here at night. Some of us climbed the bluffs back of town where we had a good view of the town. Some of the men stood guard over the teams we having heard of some of the emigrants losing horses.

Thursday, May 15. We did our trading today in this town and in the afternoon crossed the river on the ferry boat *Lizzy Baylis*. The old Missouri has the same muddy appearance here as ever. We came right through Omaha, the capitol of Nebraska. The state house is a very pretty building of brick painted white. It is situated on an eminance and can be seen from Bluff City. We camped one mile west of town on a little creek. There are a large number of campers here before us. NOTE: Stayed here till May 28th.

Friday, May 16. We are to stay some time to recruit our teams at this place. Most of the women of our company are washing. I am baking. I made some yeast bread for the first time for three weeks which tasted very good after eating hot biscuits for so long.

Saturday, May 17. Awoke this morning found it raining hard as it could pour down. The men went out of the wagon, made some coffee and warmed some beans and brought the breakfast to the wagon which we were all crowded into. Used a trunk for a table and made out a very comfortable meal. After eating we put the [dirty] dishes under the wagon where they [stayed] until four o'clock when the rain ceased and I left the shelter of the wagon for the first time today. It had grown very cold through the day, most of the men were wet through.

Sunday, May 18. The air was pure this morning but very cold. We were all shivering till about nine when the sun shone out clear and made the air much warmer. I went out with the children to take a walk and gather flowers. We went in a path through the hazel bushes, saw some hardnuts laying [on] the ground. We picked up some and cracked [them]. Finding them good gathered two quarts which were quite a luxury this time of the year. Some of the women are washing Sunday though it may be. Two gents and their ladies of our company went out horseback riding for their healths.

Monday, May 19 was fair.

Tuesday, May 20. The weather was fair this morning but towards noon it clouded up. Our company all left us to go on. We were detained waiting for a part of our company. While we are preparing our supper it began to rain so that by the time supper was ready we were slightly dampened and what was worse we had to eat in the rain.

Wednesday, May 21. Raining, yet this morning had been clear by spells but showery yet.

Thursday, May 22. Pleasant but cool and windy. Washed again today. Looking for the rest of the company.

Friday, May 23. Very warm today. Went across the brook and found some hardnuts. Also [climbed] on top of a hill from where I could overlook Council Bluffs and Omaha and the Missouri River at the ferry.

Saturday, May 24. Still waiting. No one can imagine how tiresome to wait so long in your wagon with nothing to do till they have tried it.

Sunday, May 25. Our friends have not made their appearance yet. The weather is fair today. I left Gus to keep house and went for more hardnuts gathering near two quarts. Before I came away [from where I found the nuts] Albert came and helped me. The sun shown to become very warm. It was quite a relief to get back into the wagon where we had a fine time cracking and eating nuts.

Monday, May 26. Arose this morning early. The sky was clear and the sun shone very warmly. I did quite a large washing today. Found the sun rather warm for washing-day especially where one has to be in the sun with no shade. Just as I had prepared supper and we were just about sitting down to eat, Albert looked up and said "That looks like Old Frank and that's father, I know." Sure enough, it was Father Gould and Lucy with him. I was overjoyed to see them at last. As soon as they came the men pitched the tent. We visited till near midnight.

Tuesday, May 27. We did not travel today. Stayed for the newcomers to wash and to do some shopping. In the afternoon, Lucy, Charlie, father and I went to Omaha, Lou and Charlie for the purpose of getting [photographs] taken. But the light was not good so [the photographer] was not able to take them. Father got some lemonade for the ladies. NOTE: Been here since May 16.

Wednesday, May 28. Left our encampment this morning all in good spirits and glad to be on our way. The roads were very good. Passed over some very pretty country. Nooned near a little creek. While we were eating on the ground there came along a peddler. We invited him to eat with us which he did very readily. He gave Albert a fiddle string [plausibly in exchange for the meal]. Camped late at night close to the river a half mile west of Elkhorn village. In the night there came up a very hard storm, the wind blowing fiercely for nearly two hours.

Thursday, May 29. Did not start early this morning. Traveled over some beautiful bottom land. In the forenoon we came in sight of the Platte River off to the left probably six or eight miles from us. We nooned on the prairie. Camped two miles east of Fremont.

Friday, May 30. Left our encampment about nine o'clock. We were not in a hurry on account of the rain and bad roads. While we were breakfasting this morning there was an Indian came in. He asked for something to eat. We gave him some doughnuts [and] offered him some milk which he declined. He peered around some time and finally said "coffee is good, sugar too." So I gave him some coffee with sugar in it. He took it and stirred it well and drank it leisurely with his biscuits. [When] we asked him if he was a Pawnee he said yes. Albert asked him if the Sioux were good [and] he [retorted], "Sioux no good, Cheyennes no good, Omaha good, Ottoes very good." [Then] he wanted the men to set up a piece of money for him to shoot at with his bow and arrow. Gus finally set up a three-cent piece which the Indian brought down. Nooned on the prairie. Just as we got our table set on the ground the rain began to come. We moved it so [to be] partially sheltered. We were somewhat dampened before we finished our dinner. The rain ceased before it was time to go, so Lou and I shot at a mark with a revolver. The boys said we did first rate for beginners. Camped at night at North Bend on the bank of the Platte. There was an Indian wigwam near where we stopped. We say twenty or thirty Indians, some squaws and one little papoose.

Saturday, May 31. Passed over level country near the Platte. Nooned near a little creek called in the guide book Shell Creek. Charlie went to the creek and tried to catch a fish but could not [as] he could find no bait. Camped at night about 80 rods from a road near a house where there was a post office. Gus was fiddling in the evening and two ladies and one gent came over. Albert played some. They wished us to come up to the house and have a little dance but Albert, feeling indisposed, we declined the invitation.

Thursday, June 1. We arose early this morning and found the air very warm and pleasant. Albert was quite ill this morning and was not able to sit up much till most [of the] night [was over]. We stopped at noon to rest for the rest of the day. We went from the road about half of a mile [and] stayed near [what we took to be an abandoned] old Pawnee village. There were several Indians around [our] camp. I don't like them. These are real intelligent looking ones. We are near the Loup [River].

Monday, June 2. Came through a small town by the name of Columbus three miles from where we camped. Put some letters in the post office there. Bought a thimble. We came a mile from town to the ferry of the Loup [River which enters the Platte near Columbus]. We forded part of the way and [crossed] the rest on a rope ferry. We saw some more Indians driving ponies. Nooned on the prairie near some other emigrants, whom I think likely we will fall in company with. Camped for [the] night on the banks of Looking Glass Creek, 'twas a very pleasant place. Had a nice cold spring of water with a gravel bottom, something unusual for this part of the country. Albert went fishing and caught two fish about as long as one's finger. I cooked one for him, his appetite is rather capricious, he not being well.

Tuesday, June 3. Left our encampment early this morning. After two miles traveling came to a little long lake where we found very nice soft, clear water. We watered our teams here. There are very many beautiful islands in the Platte, mostly timbered with cottonwood, but occasionally we see some covered with cedar and some elm. I should like to have a boat so as to take a boat ride once in a while. Nooned on the banks of the Platte. On the afternoon we passed a lonely nameless grave on the prairie. It had a head-board. It called up a sad train of thoughts. To my mind it seems so sad to think of being buried and left alone in so wild a country with no one to plant a flower or shed a tear over one's grave. Camped on the Platte bottom half a mile from the road opposite to an island. We had [fire] wood which we carried with us. Found a well with good water in it.

Wednesday, June 4. Had an early start this morning. [The weather] was [very] clean, clear, bright and warm. We traveled nearly ten miles I should think [then] nooned on the Platte bank. The boys waded [over] to an island and brought [back] some [buffalo] chips in a sack. These [chips] were sufficient to cook our supper. Camped near the banks of the Platte again. Here the men partly organized [and] chose a captain. His name is Wilson. He has been through to California once before.

Thursday, June 5. Arose this morning at four o'clock therefore had an early start. Traveled ten miles. We passed another grave this forenoon. His name was on the headboard. We was buried in 1861. He was twenty years old. Have passed quite a number of good farms. We hear that this is a Mormon settlement. If there was plenty of timber this would be beautiful farming country as the farmers have a home market for all they can raise and get a good price for it too. Nooned near the river. We have seen some indications of alkali for the last two days. Have passed two or three beer shops and toward night came to a sawmill and corn mill, the latter is a government mill to grind corn for the Indians. We also saw quite a sight for this part of the world, a large two story frame house not quite done yet. Camped on the banks of Wood River a nice little stream. Went to a dance in the evening. Went two miles with horned[*sic.*] horses. Walked home. Arrived at home at twelve o'clock.

Friday, June 6. "Twas a very hard task to arouse ourselves sufficiently to [get up] this morning at 4, but we did so. The weather is beautiful. Lou and I walked some time this forenoon. While we were walking we saw four graves in an enclosure. They all looked

as if they had been made at the same time. There
being a house near, we stopped to the door and inquired
about them. Found that they were the graves of a
father and three sons who were murdered by the Indians
last February. They went to the woods for wood and
never came back. They were found dead, and teams were
gone, was supposed they were killed for the teams.
The Indians were Sioux or Cheyennes they never knew
which. Camped for night on the banks of Wood River.
Had plenty of wood. Drove the teams across the creek
for grass.

Saturday, June 7. Left our camp early this morning
over level prairie. The grass is very poor. It is of
a bluish color [and] the cattle don't eat it at all.
Nooned on the banks of Wood River again near a house.
The little boys went into the creek bathing. Camped
for the night on the Platte. McBerridge took the
spade and dug a hole for water which was soon filled
with water much clearer and better than the Platte
water. We washed some.

Sunday, June 8. Our cattle were well rested. Did
not start till one o'clock today. This camp is a
little above opposite to Fort Kearney. We heard the
night and morning gun. We were in sight of the flag
yesterday. The river is so high that we were unable
to get across although we were very anxious to, to get
letters. The road this afternoon has been through
where there were many prairie dog knolls making the
road more uneven than is usual for this country. We
crossed two deep dry ravines. Camped near a small
creek, got some willows for wood. The water is very
poor. There were three wagons of emigrants camped
when we got here.

Monday, June 9. There is quite a high south wind
this morning which makes very disagreeable traveling
on account of the dust. No rain for some time and so
much travel on the road, beats up the earth into dust.
Nooned on the banks of Buffalo Creek. The men shot a

skunk near by the camp which was not very agreeable to the campany generally. Prepared for the storm but none came.

Tuesday, June 10. Did not start very early. Albert and one of the other boys went in pursuit of some antelope that they saw. [They] walked five miles, joined us on the road where we watered our teams. One of Capt. Wilson's cows got in to a slough. Went 18 miles without water or food for our teams. Did not get dinner for ourselves. Some of us ate a cracker and some did not. Had to turn off the road four or five miles to get to the river where we camped for the night. The boys played around till dark. There were signs of rain [but the boys] went to bed [without staking down their tent. They] called to Albert to come stake down the tent. I tried to get him not to do it but he [got up and] would [anyway]. We finally did have a very hard storm [with] thunder and lightning real hard [but we] did not get much wet. Albert stood guard but had on a rubber coat so did not suffer from the rain. The grass is very poor. It is supposed to have been run out by the buffalo.

Wednesday, June 11. Did not start early on account of the ground being so wet and muddy. Traveled within a mile or two of the river all of the forenoon. Nooned on the prairie near a slough where the teams had good food and drink. Lou and I went calling on a new neighbor who has a sick child. Have been near the river most of the time since noon. Pitched our tent within a few feet of the river. The sky was very clear when we went to bed but about one o'clock the wind began to blow, had quite a hard blow but no rain.

Thursday, June 12. Left early this morning. Traveled three miles when we came to some low sandy bluffs which [met] the river's [edge]. We came through a good deal of water, the Platte being high it had run over the road. I had to drive. When I came to some quite deep water, the camp kettle floated off—the watering pail also. I caught the kettle with the whipstalk but the pail was too far back for me to catch so I left it for Gus to pick up. The road was very sandy and hard for the teams across the bluffs. Here we found a new kind of flower which is very pretty. Nooned near the river, had excellent grass for the beasts. Passed three graves this afternoon. One of them has a silk handkerchief put on the end of a stick, which was placed at the head of this grave. The man was shot accidentally last month. Camped at night on the prairie near a slough. Got water from a hold dug in the ground.

Friday, June 13. This morning when we started I should think there were a hundred teams in sight at one time. There were three large companies camped close by where we [camped]. We left our [campsite] early. The weather was very warm. After two miles of travel, we came to the nicest spring of cold water I ever saw. The water in the midst of white sand [the pool was] eight feet across [and ran into] quite a large creek. Had very good roads. Crossed Carrion Creek. A lady in our train was thrown from her horse and injured quite severely. [The men] sent a mile ahead for a doctor who was in the next train. Camped on the Platte banks. [We] were threatened with a storm but [got] only a few drops of rain. Used buffalo chips [to cook our supper].

Saturday, June 14. 'Twas not very early when we started this morning. We had several sloughs to cross when we first started and after that we came to very sandy, low bluffs which we passed over. Nooned in the midst of them where we found a pond of water and some poor feed for the cattle. We see more cactus today than we have seen before. Yesterday we passed the junction of the two Plattes, the north and the south [forks]. We followed the North [Fork] on the north side [of the river]. Had a better road in the afternoon. Wind blew very hard. Camped on the banks of

North Bluff [*sic*] Fork to stay over Sunday [where] there was a large encampment. Had quite a blow just after we [finished washing the] supper dishes.

Sunday, June 15. We did not rise very early this being Sunday. Did our washings in the afternoon [then] took our clothes to the river to rinse. This is a beautiful stream, nice sandy bottom, six rods [about 90 feet] wide and eighteen inches deep and with clear water which is quite a rarity here. Had preaching in our company this afternoon. A very good sermon. Had quite a congregation. This is the eighth day since we have seen a human habitation. Had another quite hard blow.

Monday, June 16. Had some trouble about finding our cattle this morning so we did not get started as early as we should. Traveled nearly all of the forenoon over sandy bluffs, the sandiest roads I ever saw. It is put down in the guide book as Sandy Bluff east foot. We nooned near a little creek not far from the river. We passed another lonely grave today. It was made on a bluff of sand. Had a sandy road most of the time for two days. Camped half-a-mile south of the road on the North Platte. The stream is getting much smaller now [as we are proceeding upriver].

Tuesday, June 17. We were up sometime before the sun this morning, therefore had an early start. The air was cool and pleasant. We had another range of sandy bluffs to cross this forenoon. Sand was very deep. Have crossed several beautiful creeks, very clear, saw some alkali on the ground. Mr. Neff, Charlie, and Albert went onto the side of the bluffs to shoot at some jack rabbits which we saw but did not get any. They are about twice as large as our common rabbit. The captain and his brother went in pursuit of some buffalo. Have not yet returned. We nooned near a little spring creek, a very pretty place. Crossed several nice little creeks. The banks of the south side of the river come quite down to the water.

They are somewhat rocky. This afternoon the first rocks we have seen since we left Omaha. Camped on the Platte where the banks are stony. There are some small cedar trees (the stone and trees on the south side). Went two miles for [buffalo] chips [so we could start a cooking fire].

Wednesday, June 18. There was plenty of alkali where we camped. The place was damp, low ground. When I got up this morning my shoes had a streak of saleratus clear around them. The road was somewhat sandy for a few miles. Have crossed four or five spring creeks [coming] from the bluffs. We have found some rocks on the bluffs north of the road today for the first time. On the south side, between the road and the river, the land is swampy with flags and bul-rushes growing. The bottom is not more than three miles wide here. We crossed one creek which ran at the foot of the bluffs. The banks were rather steep at the crossing and just below they were almost per-pendicular ten feet high clay banks. Nooned on the prairie without water. After going a mile-and-a-half we crossed what is called Wolf Creek at the foot of some sandy bluffs which we have to cross. They are very bad indeed, the worst road we have had yet. After crossing them we go along at the foot of the bluffs for some time. Camped for night near Watch Creek, a kind of swampy creek.

Thursday, June 19. The mosquitoes were very troublesome so it was early this morning when we arose. Lou and I walked awhile. Crossed two creeks. Passed Ash Hollow which is on the south side of the river. Here we saw a large train of emigrants come to the river. They have been in sight all day.

Oregon Trail markers at Ash Hollow near Lewellen, Nebraska are on Highway 26. Photos by Bert Webber

Crossed Castle Creek three miles west of Ash Hollow. Nooned opposite to Castle Bluffs. The bluffs look like some old castles. There is no timber yet. There are a very many small islands in the river here but they are destitute of timber. We traveled on bottom land all of the afternoon but not near the river. We kept going and going thinking to come to some creek but did not. We did not camp till sundown. By the time the teams were put out it was dark. We had no [fire] wood [except] a little dry kindling. We used that to boil some coffee and ate some crackers [then we] went to bed after the men took care of the teams. Camped on low bottom. Passed the grave of a woman who died this spring.

Friday, June 20. Did not get started as early as usual. Only crossed one creek which was Crab Creek. Saw some new kind of cactus flower. It was straw color [and] is a third larger than a wild rose. Just after we crossed Crab Creek we came to some bluffs which some of the boys climbed from whence they could see Chimney Rock which is forty miles above here on the river. Saw a notice near the road warning emigrants to take care of their cattle [as Indians in the area] had stolen 12 head. Nooned on the banks of the North Platte. Had quite a good road till we came to some sand bluffs where we found some very hard road— gravel. Camped at the foot of some bluffs that look like ancient ruins. It is called Bluff Ruins in the guide book. I never saw anything as curious. I would like to have been able to [get closer] to see them. After we camped there came up a hard thunder shower just as we were eating our supper. It did us no harm. Saw Chimney Rock from here. It looks as large as a telegraph post from here.

CHIMNEY ROCK

Rising 470 feet above the North Platte River Valley, Chimney Rock stands to the south as the most celebrated of all natural formations along the overland routes to California, Oregon, and Utah. Chimney Rock served as an early landmark for fur traders, trappers, and mountain men as they made their way from the Rockies to the Missouri River. To later emigrants, the solitary spire marked the end of plains travel and the beginning of the rugged mountain portion of their journey.

The tip of the formation is 325 feet above the base. Chimney Rock is composed of Brule Clay with interlayers of volcanic ash and Arickaree sandstone. Thousands of travelers carved their names in the soft base only to have these records disappear through the forces of nature. This eroded landmark is smaller than that which greeted early visitors to the area, but its presence for the generations of the near future is secure.

In 1941 the eighty acres containing the site were transferred to the Nebraska State Historical Society by the Roszel F. Durnal family. In 1956 Norman and Donna Brown deeded additional land to the Society. In that same year Chimney Rock was designated a National Historic Site by the federal government.

Nebraska State Historical Society

Chimney Rock is near the junction of Highways 26 and 92 near Bayard, Nebraska.

Photos by Bert Webber

Saturday, June 21. The air was very pure and cool this morning after the rain. As soon as we were fairly on the road we came in sight of Court House Rock, which can be seen fifteen or twenty miles, it is on the south side of the river nine miles from the river. We don't cross as many creeks as we have done lately. The road is sandy this forenoon. Nooned near the Platte, got water from a dug spring. In the afternoon it was very warm with a south wind. Crossed some low sandy bluffs not nearly as bad as we have crossed. Camped near the river. Prepared for the storm again. This time we got the rain—rained nearly till midnight. Passed the grave of a little girl.

Within about 10 miles are Courthouse, Jail and Chimney Rocks, all major attractions along the Old Emigrant Trail and easily seen from today's highways. (Above) Jail Rock. The small black "spot" on the east (left) side in picture is an eagles nest.   Photo by Bert Webber

Court House Rock about which Franzwa writes in his *The Oregon Trail Revisited*, "allegedly was named by emigrants who fancied it resembled the courthouse in St. Louis [before it was] outfitted with its present tall...dome...the name came because the rock looked like a court house—any courthouse." Mattes, in his *The Great Platte River Road* quotes several sources including Rufus Sage on his trek with trappers in 1841: "It stands as the proud palace of Solitude amid boundless domains." Often times the "jail," in towns, was next to the court- house thus the rock formation immediately adjacent has been called Jail House Rock.

Photo by Bert Webber

Sunday, June 22. Did not start till late. The weather is warm but the roads are not dusty. The grass is not good here or has it been for several days. Charley's team got [up]set this morning. One of the bow keys came out and one of the cows became unyoked in the slough. The alkali is very strong and very plentiful in this section of the country. Our road has been on lowland today but not wet generally. Nooned nearly opposite to Chimney Rock. Have come in sight of the telegraph posts again on the south side of the river. We have found lately some very pretty varieties of flowers, among which are some which look very much like white poppies. Another kind is a white primrose. Our road is not good this afternoon. Full of ruts. Went off from the road some way to camp. We are near two traders who live in a tent made of buffalo skins. They had some squaws living with them. We saw some of their half-breed papooses [which are] cunning. There was an old Indian Chief with his family lived near them. He and his squaw came to see us. He had a paper stating that he was a good Indian and friendly to whites. His name was Long Chin, well named too. He showed us his likeness which he had taken when he was in Washington. He said "many squaws shake hands when in Washington." Charlie has just had his hair shingled. The old chief rubbed his hand over Charlie's head and said, "Pawnee, Pawnee no good." then laughed. The Pawnees have their heads sheared mostly. Rained last night.

Monday, June 23. It was somewhat cloudy this morning when we arose. Had a rough road this forenoon. Stopped for noon near the Platte. It is filled with small islands. The boys have gone bathing. There is the grave of a woman near here, the tire of a wagon is bent up and put up for a head and foot stone, her name and age is filed upon it. Turned off the road to a small creek where we found a good spring of water, quite a rarity nowadays. The name of the creek is Spring Creek. We passed another trading post in the

Some members of the Oregon-California Trails Association visited
the grave of Rebecca Winters on a
field trip during an annual convention at Scottsbluff in 1985.
Burlington-Northern track in fore-
ground.   Photo by Bert Webber

Rebecca Winters, a Mormon pioneer
age 50, died along the trail of
cholera. When railroad surveyors
discovered the grave, which was
marked with a bent wagon tire,
they changed the route of the
track to miss the grave.
          Photo by Gregory M. Franzwa
     from *The Oregon Trail Revisited*

afternoon. We were visited by some Indians [including] a squaw with her papoose on her back. [She] had some game to sell. We were frying some meat [when] the little fellow reached out his hand. We have him some crackers which he ate very eagerly. Had a small shower in the evening.

Tuesday, June 24. Were up rather rate this morning but had a choice breakfast of antelope steak which was brought by Mr. Bullwinkle [of] some that he'd bought of the Indians. He brought it for us to cook on shares. It was really delicious. We passed through a small temporary Indian village this afternoon. We saw that they had over one hundred ponies. There were sixteen wigwams. The road was better today. Nooned on the Platte banks. While we were eating our lunch an Indian Chief rode up on a nice mule. His bridle was covered with silver plates—Masonic emblems. He, the Indian, was dressed in grand style. He had a looking glass and comb suspended by a string, had a fan, and silver ornaments made of half dollars into fancy shapes. I can't describe half the ornaments that he wore. He was real good looking for an Indian. He wore earrings as much as eight inches long made of clamshells, beads, and silver.

We came near some rocks on the north side of the road in the side of some bluffs, the first rocks we have seen close by since we left the Missouri. Georgie, Frank, and I went to them. I put some small stones in some of the crevices. The river was near on the south. Camped on the banks of the Platte. There we found timber for the first time for two hundred miles. It was really refreshing to see [trees] once more. The cattle thought so too I guess for as soon as they were unyoked they each went to a tree and began to rub. Saw Laramie Peak today for the first time.

Wednesday, June 25. We had an early start this morning. The road was sandy and the day warm. Nooned on the Platte banks near some timber. They drove the

cattle across to an island [but] when they went for
them [the men] were obligated to disrobe and swim for
them. The Indians came around, so many that we hardly
had a chance to get our dinners. They were very
anxious to "swap" moccasins and lariats for money,
powder, and whiskey but we had [no whiskey] to trade.
Charlie traded a little iron teakettle for a lariat.
Two of them shot at a mark with Albert's gun with
Albert; he beat them. Our road this afternoon was
quite sandy. The wind blew hard towards night which
made it very disagreeable for our eyes. Camped on the
bank of the Platte opposite an island close by a
company of seven teams. Our men guarded with the
other company.

Thursday, June 26. Did not get a very early start.
Our road was quite sandy. The bottom land was made
yellow with the blossoms of the wild sunflower and
dotted with white primrose. We have been in sight of
timber all day. Passed a little squad of Indian tents.
There was a blacksmith shop kept by a white man. Met
a light covered wagon filled with squaws and half-breed
children. Nooned a mile above Fort Laramie on the
opposite side of the river. We found no feed for our
teams so [the men] did not unyoke them although we
stayed there for hours for a man to go [to the fort]
for our letters. He had to pay a dollar for being
taken over in a skiff. It took five to ten minutes to
go over in the low water. There is a ford [but too
deep for our wagons]. We were very much disappointed
at not being able to go over and see the fort. There
was an Indian being buried in a tree close to where we
nooned. He was wrapped in a buffalo robe. He was
laid on some sticks on branches of a tree and had been
[up] there but a few days. There are acres of wild
roses. They are really beautiful. The man got back
with our letters. [Fort Laramie is Wyoming's first
post office having been established in 1850.] We had
two [letters]. We went four miles up the river and
camped. Had a very nice place for camping but not

very good feed. We guarded our teams with another
company.

Friday, June 27. Had a very early start this morning, began climbing hills and kept doing so all day.
They are part of the Black Hills. We nooned on the
side [of a] hill. Had to drive the cattle half-a-mile
for water. Had but very little for ourselves in the
can. The hills are partly covered with pine and cedar.
While we were nooning a man came along and told us
there was a spring only a mile-and-a-half ahead of us.
We were all very very thirsty, indeed. When we got
there we found twenty to thirty teams getting drinking
water. There were two springs but very small so it
was slow work filling our cans. We traveled up and
down some of the steepest hills that I ever saw, but
I suppose they are only a beginning to what we shall
have to go over. Had to lock both hind wheels to the
wagon. We saw a grave on top of one of the lower
hills. The road is rough and stony most of the way
today. There is plenty of nice dry wood, pine and
cedar. It looks very tempting after going so long
without it. Only found drinking water once in our
day's travel. Camped on the Platte banks again.
There were, I should think, nearly a hundred wagons.
The men had to drive the cattle a mile-and-a-half for
food. They kept them there all of the time. Had a
day and night guard. Albert and the Captain had to go
the first night with the others. They took blankets
and two slept while two guarded. There is a blacksmith shop in a skin tent and for a wonder no Indians
around. Only four squaws.

Saturday, June 28. Did not travel today. Stayed
over to let the cattle have a chance to rest. Albert
set the tire of his wagon wheels and set some shoes on
the horses which made a pretty hard day's work for him.
He also shortened the reach of his wagon. The smith
here only charged ten dollars for shoeing a yoke of
oxen. I did a large washing and Lucy did a large
quantity of cooking, made herself nearly sick working

so hard. Gus and I took my clothes to the river to
rinse. There was a little island covered with wild
rose bushes near by. Gus tried to wade over to it to
hand the clothes but it was too deep so we were obliged
to hang them on some low bushes close by the river.

Monday, June 30. We did not start very early. The
sky was clear this morning. Crossed the creek back
again. There was a trader and his squaws near the
creek. When we first started we followed up a deep
ravine. There was a short distance where the rocks
were perpendicular with pine and cedar growing on the
left side of the road. Our road is sandy this forenoon, crossed a kind of a run. Nooned on the prairie.
Had a very good road in the afternoon. There were
some curious piles of gravel and cobble stones making
quite large hills. Crossed a dry run with timber on
it. Camped on the river bank near some cottonwoods.

Tuesday, July 1. Arose very early this morning.
It was very foggy. When they went for the cattle,
some were not to be found but by going over the bluff
they found them. In the night I heard Mrs. Wilson's
baby crying very hard [as the baby] had fallen from
the wagon. He struck on his head. It cried nearly an
hour. Crossed two runs this afternoon, one was quite
good size but very muddy. The road is good. Nooned
on the river bank again. Had real good grass. Rather
rough sandy road in the afternoon. Turned off the
road half-a-mile to get to the river. Had a very good
camping place. The water in the river keeps getting
clearer and some colder. Came through some very steep
and unshapely bluffs. There was scarcely any vegetation on them. Some of the men climbed one very steep
one on the left of the road. When they were on it
they looked no larger than three or four year old boys.
There were great seams in the bluffs caused by the
rains I suppose, which made them look like columns to
some building.

Wednesday, July 2. Arose before the sun this morning. There was a man in the company who is traveling with us who hurt himself wrestling so badly that when he first got up he thought he would be unable to ride but after awhile he thought he would try it and did so. We came for a short distance on level land, but soon came to the hills which were most abrupt and dreary looking things I ever saw. It seems as if there had been some grand convulsion of nature which had turned everything topsy-turvy. We traveled all of the forenoon over the hills to get a few miles. The river is very crooked, not nearly so straight as it is nearer the mouth. We nooned close by the river on a little flat of a few acres. The grass is tolerably good but has been trampled over a great deal. We [lit] a campfire and made some coffee which we do not usually make for dinner. Camped on the Platte after a short afternoon's drive. Traveled on the river bottom. The ground where we stayed was covered with spear grass and cactus, therefore was not very pleasant to walk on.

Thursday, July 3. Had an early start. Lou and I walked awhile this morning but could not [go] far on account of the roads being sandy. Nooned near the river again. Had a short rest, traveled all day, raised up with some strange grains. It is very inconvenient to be with so many for we got on so slow. There are so many more stoppages. There came up quite a hard blow towards night before we were camped and being among sand hills we were well showered with sand if not with rain. Blew quite hard just at sundown but did not trouble us much. To the left of us, as we were coming, between us and the river there was a sand hill which had no vegetation on it. Looked very singular. Camped near the river.

Friday, July 4. Today is the Fourth of July and here we are away off in the wilderness and can't even stay over a day to do any extra cooking. The men fired their guns. We wonder what the folks at home are doing and Oh! how we wish we were there. Albert

is not well today so I drive. I have been in the
habit of sleeping awhile every forenoon so naturally
I was sleepy driving. Went to sleep a multitude of
times to awaken with a start fancying we were running
into gullies. After going a short distance we came in
sight of a mail station on the other side of the river.
There were several buildings of adobe I suppose.
Nearly opposite on this side of the river we passed a
little log hut which is used for a store. It was
really a welcome sight after going four hundred miles
without seeing a house of any kind. Passed also some
Indian tents with white men and squaws [being the]
dwellers therein. Our road was level but sandy, not
much grass. Had a light shower. Camped near the
river. Did not turn off the road.

Saturday, July 5. We were aroused this morning
early by the guard calling out that there was a dead
cow in the camp. The boys went out and to our dismay
found it to be one of Charlie's. They did not know
what was the matter. They opened her up [but did not
learn anything]. Some thought it was the murrain and
some thought she was alkalied. Had a great time getting down a steep hill near the river. There were near
two hundred wagons collected at the top all trying to
go first. It took nearly two hours for them all to
get down. There was another road at the foot of the
hill but it was very muddy. Passed a bridge across the
N. Platte built by the Mormons. Toll: 50 cents. The
Scott train [from] Des Moines crossed over to avoid the
big sand hill. We nooned on the Platte banks. Traveled
most of the afternoon through the sand bluffs, passed
by another bridge six miles above the other. Here is
where the stage passes also the telegraph wire. It
seems pleasant to have it by the road side again. At
the bridge is a mail station. Camped on the river again.

Sunday, July 6. Stayed over to wash and cook and
recruit the cattle. [It was] a very pleasant place
[but we] had quite a blow in the afternoon. Camped
on the Platte for the last time.

Monday, July 7. Started very early this morning traveled near the river for eight miles, [then] came to the Red Buttes which are on the north side of the river. We go a short distance past these and come to Willow Spring Creek. At the crossing is a station and a good spring. After we left this, we came to no water but alkali for 15 miles or did we find feed. The road was very rough and some of the way stony. Camped for night at sundown at the head of a little creek where we found excellent water in a spring and good grass. Came over Prospect Hill from whence we can see the Sweetwater Mountains. Camped a mile-and-a-half beyond.

Tuesday, July 8. Left our encampment at seven. The air is very pure here so near the mountains. After going a mile and a half we came to a very nice brook. The road in the forenoon was good, followed a small creek for a mile, six miles farther we came to Greasewood Creek where there is a mail station. The keeper's wife had just come from the east. I should think it would be very lonely living so far from anyone. They are going to Red Butte Station to keep an eating house. Nooned on the prairie on very poor grass. In the afternoon came to the alkalie springs and swamps. The ground is covered with saleratus. I dipped up some of the water and put some acid in it. It foamed up to fill the cup. Here is where the Mormons gather their saleratus. Some of our company saved some [but] it looked rather dirty. It is best to tie all of the cattle that are not in the yoke for fear of them drinking this water. I tasted some of it. It was so strong as any lye I ever saw. Came to a mail station here. There are stationed ninety troops. We stayed some time and conversed with them. There is a bridge across the Sweetwater [River]. Some cross the bridge and some go up six miles and cross on another. There were four teams of us crossed here and the rest went up the other side of Independence Rock. This rock is six hundred yards long and forty

INDEPENDENCE ROCK

Here are measurements as provided by various writers.

Jane Gould's diary
600 yards long   40 yards high

Ellison's book*
1,522 yards circumference
                    193 feet high—north end
                    167 feet high—south end
                     60 feet high at center

Haines' book*
1,900 feet long   700 feet wide
            128 feet maximum relief above
            the valley floor

Webster's Geographical Dictionary (1972)
1,950 feet long   850 feet wide
            193 feet high—north end

U.S.Geological Survey (1870)
1,550 yards circumference
                    193 feet high—north end
                    167 feet high—south end

Beware of rattlesnakes in area.

Franzwa calls the rock, "a great black scarred turtle shell bulging from the flat plain. "*

---

*see bibliography

Independence Rock on the Sweetwater River, Wyoming
Photo by Bert Webber

high. We were in plain sight of it. We paid half-a-
dollar toll across the bridge just opposite where the
rest of our train were camped. Had very good grass
and water from the Sweetwater.

Wednesday, July 9. Our road passes within half a
mile of the Devil's Gate which is six miles above
Independence Rock. We turned from the road and went
to see it. I will give the John C. Fremont's description of it, which will be more correct than I
can give:

> Five miles above the rock is a place
> called the Devil's gate where the
> Sweetwater cuts through the point of
> a granite ridge. The length of the
> passage is about three hundred yards
> and the width thirty-five yards. The

walls of rock are vertical and about
four hundred feet in height and the
stream in the gate is almost entirely
chocked up by masses which have fallen
from above. In the wall on the right
bank is a dike of traprock cutting
through a fine grained gray granite.

The water runs through the gate in a torrent, all over
the rocks where they are smooth, are names written,
some up twenty feet. As we were coming back [from our
walk to the wagon] we wrote our names on some rocks.
Nearly half-a-mile down from the gate Lucy and Charlie
wrote theirs and I wrote mine and Georgie's and
Frankie's on a rock on the right side of the road.
Albert wrote his name farther up. After getting on
the main road we came through between two rocky
bluffs. After some time, crossed a small creek, the
water was not clear. Crossed another [creek] where
there is a mail station. We see perfect clouds of
grasshoppers! We have seen, for the past week, some
pretty new flowers among which are the wild blue lark-
spurs which are much prettier than those we cultivate
in our gardens. We hear many stories of Indian depredations but we do not feel frightened yet. Passed
the station which was built in the place of one that
was burned where two men were murdered in the spring.
Nooned on the Sweetwater. Had to drive the cattle
over the river to feed. Our road was good mostly on
the river bottom. All the vegetation is sage brush
and greasewood or more properly speaking, absinthe.
Camped alone near no other camp. It is not considered
perfectly safe for a small train to travel alone after
we get a little farther up the river. Crossed a
little creek on a bridge. Paid five cents toll. The
alkali was very plenty at our camping place. When the
men drove the cattle down to drink the cattle went and
swam the river. Stayed till after sundown when three
of the men had to swim after them. It had got to be
very cool and they were obliged to be there [quite a]

time getting [the cattle] together. When they got
[back home the men] were very cold. Rained some.
Had to use sage brush for [fire]wood.

Thursday, July 10. Did not get started very early.
The road is very sandy. On the opposite side of the
river to us the mountains are just huge masses of
granite. Some of them have a few stunted pines growing from the crevices. We can see snow in the mountains now. Those on the south of us are timbered with
pine. We passed the grave of a man who was shot by
his partners. They were emigrants. They had a quarrel
and Young shot Scott dead. The company had a trial
and found him guilty and gave him his choice of being
hung or shot. He preferred being shot, and was forth-
with. Nooned on the bank of the river. The road is
somewhat sandy, no vegetation but sage brush and
greasewood. Camped on the Sweetwater near two other
large parties of emigrants. There was a wedding in
one of the camps adjoining ours. The couple came up
to our camp to get our minister to marry them. They
had closed doors to the tent while the ceremony was
being performed.

Friday, July 11. Had a very good road in the forenoon. Passed by a station occupied by soldiers who
are placed here for the protection of the emigrants.
The station is close to the banks of the river. There
was a little child run over by a wagon in Walker's
train who are just ahead of us. The child was injured
quite seriously. They sent for a German physician
that belonged to our train to see the child. The
doctor said he thought the child would get better.
There is a ford to the river here at this station but
the water is so high we were unable to cross and
therefore have some bad sand hills to go over. We
passed between two high ranges of rock bluffs that are
quite near each other. On the rocks nearest the road
are written many names. We left ours. Came in sight
of the Windrivers Mountains covered with snow. Found

no chance to feed at noon. Camped on the banks of the Sweetwater near Walker's train.

Saturday, July 12. Left our camp early this morning. Had a good road but quite hilly. Found no feed for our cattle at noon but we stopped long enough to eat lunch and for the men to exchange some pork for some beef with soldiers who were stationed nearby. Mr. Church has a very sick ox. Is obliged to yoke his cow with an ox. We traveled till after dark before we found grass and water. Passed by the ice springs. The Captain dug down a few inches and they got a pail full of ice on the 12th of July. Our encampment is on the Sweetwater again. [NOTE : Maps of the area indicate the party was probably at about 6,500 feet altitude.]

Sunday, July 13. Did not travel today but washed, baked, cooked beef, stewed peaches, boiled corn. We had an excellent feed, the best we have had for some time. There were several soldiers came to call on us. Some of the boys to fix the ford [in the river].

Monday, July 14. Started early this morning. Crossed the river at an old ford, the water was pretty high but did not run into the wagon box. The road has been rather hilly this forenoon. Nooned on the Sweetwater with Walker's train. Did not travel in the afternoon. There were some soldiers stationed near us. We gave them a pail of milk. In the night there were two [soldiers] who deserted and took two of the best army horses. They are supposed to have gone west.

Tuesday, July 15. Did not start early this morning. Joined Walker's train last night so now we are in a train of [about] 73 wagons. The road had been hilly this afternoon and sometimes rocky. Took dinner by a little lake. We are getting to such an altitude that the air is quite rare and I, for one, feel rather more lazy than usual. One of the train just came in with a large antelope. The boys saw some snow drifts off to the left of the road. Some of the boys brought some

[snow] down for a rarity to look at. That night we camped within twenty rods of probably a thousand tons of snow. 'Twas on a creek called Strawberry Creek [south-central Fremont County, Wyoming]. There was excellent grass. We came in sight of Table Rock this afternoon.

Wednesday, July 16. Our roads were real good this forenoon. Came to the Sweetwater at noon, did not travel any farther. Found first rate grass, did some baking, drove the cattle over to the river. Had a good spring to water. There was a station of soldiers near us. We find several kinds of very pretty flowers, a number of kinds of mosses. One has a very pretty white flower and is very fragrant like the fragrance of the grass pink.

Thursday, July 17. Left our camp early. Have had a good road. Crossed two little creeks. Nooned on the last one. [Here it is middle of summer but] the weather is so cold that I really suffer [even] with a blanket around me. The Wind River mountains are to the right of us half-covered with snow. The road this afternoon has been very hilly and rocky. Have crossed several small mountain brooks with nice grass on them. The ford over the creek in the hills was washed away. A train that went before us built a bridge so we crossed on it. Camped by a small creek. It was nearly sundown but we had good feed and water.

Friday, July 18. When we arose this morning, there was a heavy white frost on the ground. It seemed cold enough to be winter. I don't see how anything can grow here. We seem to be nearer the mountains today. The road is quite good, [better than] we supposed it would be crossing the Rocky Mountains. Nooned in a little valley where we had the best of feed. The men found two or three good wagons, some harnesses, scythes, a stove, and a great many things else in a ravine off half-a-mile from the road. One man took two wagons and another a harness [all found here].

In the afternoon we passed the [South Pass] summit.
[NOTE: Elevation 7,550 feet above sea level.] We
came over the side of a small mountain through some
timber. We found several kinds of new flowers, some
of them very pretty. We had quite a steep hill to
come down after crossing the mount[ain]. One of the
train broke an axel tree to his wagon [while going]
down. After coming down the hill we came alongside
of one of the Sandy's, the water of which runs to the
Pacific. Camped on a hillside. Had to pitch our
tents among the sage brush.

Saturday, July 19. Saw this morning the Green
River Mountains for the first time. Traveled three
or four miles when we crossed the Sandy, it is a nice
little stream. The road was sandy all of the forenoon.
Camped at one o'clock and stayed the rest of the day.
Had good feed down on the bottom of a creek called
Spring Creeks. Our tent was among the sage and sand
again. Rained a little at sundown.

Sunday, July 20. Left our encampment for a twenty
miles drive without water. The road was sandy most of
the way. There was some grass in among the sage in
some places but there being no water we did not stop
at noon. Arrived at Green River about three o'clock.
Here the feed was not good but better than none.
There was one large camp above us and one below us on
the river. The timber, I think, is elm. The men had
a ball play towards night, seemed to enjoy themselves
very much. It seemed like old times. The Captain
sent a man down to a ferry that was ten miles below us
on the river to see about crossing. The charge was
four dollars per wagon and swim our own cattle and
have to wait for our turn to come.

Monday, July 21. Our men went to work this morning to build a raft. Worked hard all day. Half of
the men worked in the water. After getting it done
they had no ropes strong enough to work it across.
As the current was so swift and the water so deep

When John C. Fremont passed this way in 1842, he described South Pass as being without any "toilsome ascents." The pass is hardly a narrow cut in lofty peaks, but is a plain nearly 30 miles wide and over 100 miles long on an "imperceptible grade" (Haines) from the east. Photograph faces east from today's visitor area on Highway 28 a little west of the pass.
Photo by Bert Webber

CHRONOLOGY OF SOUTH PASS

1812   Discovery of South Pass by Robert Stuart and his group of Astorians

1826   First crossing of the pass by a wheeled vehicle

1832   First wagon train crossing led by Captain B. L. E. Bonneville of U.S. Army

1836   Narcissa Whitman and Eliza Spalding were first white women to cross South Pass

1843   Beginning of great migration

1847   First wave of Mormon pioneers

1849-51   Peak period of emigration to the American west

1860   Pony Express passed through South Pass during its nineteen months of existence

they lost a good share of their ropes. Towards night
they looked over the wagons and selected two boxes
(one of them being Charley's) to caulk for boats. The
Captain gathered up all of the resin and tar he could
and worked till eleven o'clock at night. I washed
today.

Tuesday, July 22. Went to work this morning as
early as possible ferrying the wagons. Had to take
them apart and float the box and cover behind. The
two boxes were fastened together by the rods, one
before to row in and the other to load. Worked till
dark. Got some of our groceries wet. Some sugar got
dissolved. We were the last, but one other, to cross
tonight.

Wednesday, July 23. Did not all get across yesterday. Went to work soon after sunrise and worked till
noon before the last one got across. Most of the men
had to wade in the edge of the river to tow the boat
up. Last night there were four horses and one mule
stolen from our train and ten from the next train
above us. Some of the men hunted all day and part of
the night but without success. Albert, Gus, Annie
McMillin and myself went gooseberrying but only got a
few. The mosquitoes were [big and] thick.

Thursday, July 24. Started before daylight without
our breakfast so as to get to the ferry which is six
miles, before another large train. There we [were]
obliged to wait and that in a very poor place. The
road was very rough between the two branches [of the
river]. Several steep descents and some big rocks to
go over. Gus is not well today. Albert went fishing
but caught none. Some of the other train caught some
fine trout. Afternoon: We got the use of the boat in
time to bring over fourteen wagons tonight. The boat
is an old scow. It is large enough to take a wagon
and load over, swim the cattle and horses. Each train
pays four dollars for it and the last man sells it to
the next one back so they all get their pay till it

comes to the last train who will [not get his] four
dollars but he did get across in good shape for a
reasonable price.

Friday, July 25. All of the teams came over today
by noon. Had no bad luck this time. Started on our
way as soon as they all came over. The road was quite
sloughy for a mile then sandy and hilly for eight
miles. After going six miles we came to a little
creek where the men watered the teams but there was
no grass near. Came two miles farther to a beautiful
creek with fine feed on the east side. We came on to
the west side but had to drive the cattle over the
other side again [then] pitch our tents in the sage
brush. It is sage ,sage, sage, scarcely anything but
sage. It burns [hot, fast] fire.

Saturday, July 26. Started early this morning and
as we went up the hill found we had stayed all night
where there had been a fight [with Indians] just a few
days ago. The Indians had taken horses from some
emigrants who in trying to recover them one man lost
his life and two others were severely wounded. The
grave is on the left side of the road as you go up the
hill. He was killed on 18th of July 1862. The road
has been dusty and rough. Did not stop till about
two, when we camped for the [rest of the] day and
night on a creek in a canyon of the mountains. Had
good grass. Annie McMillin had lagged behind walking
when we stopped. The whole train had crossed the
creek before they thought of her. The creek was so
deep that it ran into the wagon boxes so she could
not wade. A man on horseback went over for her and
another man on a mule went to help her on. The mule
refused to go clear across, went where the water was
very deep, threw the man off and almost trampled on
him, but he finally got out safe only well wet and
with the loss of a good hat, which is no trifling loss
here. We hear great stories about the Indians here
again. The scenery of the Green River Mountains is
more interesting than that of the Wind River Chain,

snow, pine forests, ledges of red sandstone and valleys of green grass over the surface. The children, Annie, and I went strawberrying. Got enough to put in cream for breakfast. I find these mountains are the Bear River Mountains instead of the Green River Chain.

Sunday, July 27. We commenced our journey this morning by starting up a canyon following up a creek which we crossed twelve times in ten miles which is the length of the canyon. Several crossings the water came into the wagon box. The roads were the worst I ever saw. The creek is unusually high as that the road is mostly muddy. Some of the wagons got [stuck]. The road washed away in many places so we have to go where we can. There is one place where the road goes for over a mile over rocks from two inches to two feet large with no gravel or soil between. It was horribly rough. There were two wagons broken down in the train just ahead of us. I expected every minute to see our old, light wagon go to pieces but it survived the day's journey. We ate snow as often as we wanted it. I saw the little ditty of the "three little boys a sliding went all on one summer day" verified. The little boys were sliding down a slide hill of snow drift. We had to go over one side hill so sliding that the men had to fasten a strong rope to the wagon and six men hold on to it on the uphill side to keep it from tipping over. Traveled ten miles and camped in a pine forest near some other emigrants. One of our train broke the axletree of his wagon. Had to repair it partly by [light of our] campfire. There was a log hut [near] where we camped.

Monday, July 28. Came for quite a number of miles through the forest of pine, spruce, and fir. Such beautiful trees as the firs are with their purple balls at the top. The top runs up to a point. I would like to have some of them in a dooryard. Had some very steep hills to ascend and descend. A person would think to look for one across to another that it was

impossible to go up them. We are crossing and re-
crossing creeks most all of the time. Came past a
camp of thirty six wagons (Kennedy train) who have
been camped for some time here in the mountains.
They have had their cattle stampeded four or five
times. A woman died in their train yesterday. She
left six children and one of them only two days old.
Poor little thing it had better have died with its
mother. They made a good picket fence around the
grave. This same train had a man accidentally shot
down at Independence Rock. They seem to be very
unfortunate. We stopped in a little valley about
two o'clock, stayed over night, had to drive the
cattle a mile back on the road to a small patch of
grass bounded on one side by a large snow drift. We
had to drive through a snow drift today.

Tuesday, July 29. Commenced climbing the mountains
again this morning. Passed a grave on the side of a
mountain. It was the grave of a man that was supposed
to have been killed by the Indians. There was an
arrow with blood on the point lying beside the grave.
He was only buried about six inches under the ground.
The Maple train ahead of us opened the grave. The
[dead] man had a bullet hole through his temple. They
found another new grave a little way from that back
in the woods. This is the place of all places for the
doing of foul deeds with its deep ravines and gorges
and thick forests. We found some beautiful flowers in
among the mountains, among others is a beautiful white
honeysuckle very much like those we raise in our
gardens only larger. We traveled from morning till
night till after dark without stopping. Came into a
valley and camped near three other large trains.
There were three wagons in our train broken today.
As our ox team was going through a creek just going
out the bank was very steep, the oxen slipped. One
of them got over the tongue to the wagon. The men
were troubled some about getting the [oxen] off so

[the men] fastened the chain to the end of the wagon and drew it out [of the creek].

Wednesday, July 30. Did not start till late. Went ten miles down the valley and camped on a creek. Had very good grass. Gus went and got some yellow currants. They were very good when stewed. We had to be very careful in looking them over. Some with black spots have worms.

Thursday, July 31. Did not leave our camp till [late]. Traveled six miles over level ground down the same valley, encamped by a creek, had the best grass we have seen on the road since Omaha. Mostly bunch grass. It was nearly sundown when we got there. I did a large washing.

Friday, August 1. Left camp in the morning, traveled six miles again and camped at the mouth of the canyon that we are to follow up. Lou and I mended and baked and made blancmanage (white pudding).

Saturday, August 2. Commenced our journey over the mountain again this morning. Our teams feel considerably refreshed after the last four days recruiting. The road in the forenoon was not bad for canyon roads, followed up a creek, crossed it five times in going five miles, we now came to the salt springs. We picked some crystalized salt which had formed on the stones on the edges of the creek. The water is as salty as any brine could be. A person could pick up a good many pounds in a day. We went over two hills and came to some more salt springs. There were acres of ground just white with it. Nooned a short time near a little creek in a ravine. We have found ice on the water nearly every morning. People coming should have woolen stockings, the men drawers and undershirts, the women warm socks and gloves or mittens, the children good shoes and stockings, overcoats and comforts. Frankie has lost his raglan [sweater]. Came through the mountains, did not get into camp till after sundown. The mountain roads today are not near as bad

as they were over the other spur. Camped in a valley
on a creek. There is not much snow on the mountains
now. We have a great deal of dust.

Sunday, August 3. We did not get a very early
start this morning on account of our hard day's drive
yesterday. We are traveling down the valley today.
It is called Large Grass Valley. It is somewhat hilly
but excellent roads. Nooned near the creek. We hear
the Kennedy train had another stampede. Afternoon:
We passed by the train I have just spoken of. They
had just buried the baby of the woman who died a few
days ago and were just digging a grave for another
woman who [just] died. She was run over by the cattle
and wagons when they stampeded yesterday. She lived
twenty-four hours. She gave birth to a child a short
time before she died. The child was buried with her.
She leaves a little two year old girl and a husband.
They say he is nearly crazy with sorrow. The Captain
of this Kennedy train is the man who arrested [the man
named] Young who had murdered Scott and ordered Young
to be shot. Young did not belong to this train but to
another. Some say that it is a judgment upon the
captain and his train for meddling with and depriving
a man of his life without the aid of the law. After
cattle have been frightened once or twice there is no
safety with them. Yesterday there were several loose
horses came running up when the train of cattle
started pellmell, crippled two men besides killing the
woman. They mark nearly half their camps with dead
cattle. I never supposed that cattle would run so in
yoke and hitched to a wagon. Our road is real good.
We pass to the left of a large swamp or lake. Camped
at night near a large nice spring.

Monday, August 4. We arose this morning very early
so as to get out of the way of the train back of us.
Had good roads, some hills to climb and crossed two or
three creeks. Nooned near a beautifully clear creek.
The men went down and caught some crabs to carry along
for bait to catch salmon trout with in a stream that

we shall come to tomorrow. The wind blew in our faces
in the afternoon and nearly suffocated us with dust.
The dust is worse than Indians, storms, or winds or
mosquitoes, or even woodticks. The country is somewhat hilly and destitute of timber. Camped near a
little creek where there was good grass but no wood.
We brought wood with us.

Thursday, August 5. Did not start early, waited
for a train to pass. [At this point in her diary, we
see Jane's real pleading of homesickness when she
says:] It seems today as if I must go home to father's
to see them all. [I feel] I can't wait another minute.
If I could only hear from [home] it would do some good
but I suppose I shall have to wait whether I am patient
or not. The road has been much the same as yesterday.
I suppose we shall have more dust the further we go.
If I could just have [a hot] bath! I presume there
has been no rain here for two months. Nooned near a
creek in a very dusty bad place. The grass is mostly
bunch grass here, which they say is very hearty for
the cattle and horses, the horses prefer it to other
grass. Camped on a rise of ground near where the Salt
Lake and Fort Hall [roads part] in. Had water to
bring nearly half-a-mile. Brought our wood with us.

Wednesday, August 6. Followed up a canyon through
the hills or mountains for a mile or two. Crossed
some broken land, entered another canyon, then another
yet. Albert found a few ripe service berries. They
are black when ripe. They are some of the shape of
red Kowe berries, grow on a shrub. Found a few ripe
yellow currants, they are very nice. Nooned on a
creek on a hill. Went to try to find some berries
but could not. Had good roads in the afternoon but
so dusty. Camped on the banks of a little creek, had
some grass to pitch our tent on, which is quite a
rarity nowadays.

Thursday, August 7. The road is mostly a level plain. Only traveled till noon. Stayed the afternoon at a creek. Wood was rather scarce. Some of the cattle and one horse got mired in it. The banks were very steep. Albert got his horses shod. Mr. Bradford shod them. He is a man that goes with Mr. Walker. He does not charge anything for what he does for those belonging to the train. Lou washed and I cooked.

Friday, August 8. Traveled eight miles. Went down a steep bank and came to Portneuf River [Idaho] where we ferried on two large skiffs fastened together and poles laid across. Took two wagons at a time. Paid a dollar-and-a-half apiece. Here we saw some Shoshone or Snake Indians. There were four or five Mormon wagons here trading, they sold flour to some of the train for ten dollars per hundred. Charley bought a dozen onions. [He] traded some caps for them. They sell [onions] for two cents apiece. They are brought from Salt Lake [City area]. We had onion soup for supper which was very good. The ferrymen were quite gentlemanly fellows for this part of the world. We took lunch after we crossed the river then came five miles and camped on a high bank in the sage brush. Had to bring water up a very steep bank some distance from the creek.

Saturday, August 9. Left our camp early. Came over hard country all of the forenoon. Nooned on the creek in the dust again. This morning we saw Salmon River Mountains away off as far as we could see. We are in sight of Three Buttes [about] forty-four miles from the road. Traveled over rather hilly ground. Camped in a valley near a spring that comes out of the bank. We had a good many mosquitoes.

Sunday, August 10. Traveled five or six miles when we came to Snake River. Followed it up two or three miles where we came to the American Falls. It is quite a sight. It falls over rocks. There are two or three little rock islands in [the river] which makes

it [look like] a second Niagara. We nooned there
so had time to examine it closely. Some of the men
caught some very nice trout. We stayed till two
o'clock then traveled till about four or five when
we, from the back of the train, saw those on ahead
all get out their guns. In a short time the word
came back that a train six miles on had been
attacked by the Indians and some killed and that
was cause enough for the arming. In a short time
we were met by two men. They wanted us to go a
short distance from the road and bring up two dead
men to this camp five miles ahead. Albert unloaded
his little wagon and sent Gus back with them and
about forty armed men from both trains to get them.
We learned that a train of eleven wagons had been
plundered of all that was in them and the teams
taken and three men killed. One was Mr. Bullwinkle
who left us on the 25th of last month at the crossing
of Green River. He went on with this Adams train,
was intending to wait for us but we had not over-
taken him yet. He was shot eight times. His dog
was shot four times before [the dog] would let the
[Indians] get to the wagon. The [Indians] took all
that he had in the wagon except his trunks and books
and papers. They broke open his trunks and took all
that they contained. He had six trunks. It is
supposed that the [Indians] took six thousand dollars
from him, tore the cover from his wagon. [The cover]
was oil cloth. He had four choice horses [but the]
horses ran away when Mr. Bullwinkle was shot. The
harnesses were found on the trail where they were
cut from them as they went. It was a nice silver
mounted harness. The Captain had a daughter shot
and wounded severely. This happened yesterday.
This morning a part of our train and a part of the
Kennedy train went in pursuit of the stock [which
were found] surrounded by Indians on ponies. Two
[Indians] were killed, several wounded and two
supposed to [have] been killed. They were never
found. One of those [whites] killed was Captain

Adams' son. The other was a young man in the Kennedy train. Those killed in the morning were carried to our camp. Mr. Bullwinkle and the others were buried before we got to the camp. There were one hundred and fifty wagons there and thirty-four of ours. Captain Kennedy was severely wounded. Captain Hunter of the Iowa City train was killed likewise an Indian. We camped near Snake River. We could not get George to ride after the news. He would walk and carry his loaded pistol. If there was any shooting going on he wanted to help. (George 10 years old, was son of the author—the pistol was a muzzle-loading affair).

Monday, August 11. The two men that were brought up were buried early this morning with the other three so they lie five men side by side in this vast wilderness, killed by the guns and arrows of the red demons. The chief appeared yesterday in a suit of Mr. Bullwinkle's. On the battlefield some of them had the best kind of rifles, some of them Minnie [*sic.*] rifles. We did not get started till late. Traveled twelve miles without stopping at noon. Came up several steep hills, over one creek with three little falls, one above the other. Camped on Raft River with the other trains.

Tuesday, August 12. Captain Adams' daughter died this morning from her wounds. [She] was buried in a box made of a wagon box. Poor father and mother lost one son and one daughter, all of his teams, clothing and four thousand dollars. Left dependent on the bounty of strangers. We only traveled half a day, camped on a creek, had the best of feed. Two or three other trains stayed also. We have just heard that there has been a train waylaid on the Oregon road. There are two trains going to California that started for Oregon. Lou wished [——the thought is incomplete, just the two words.] In the evening we took in Mrs. Ellen Jones one of the ladies of the plundered train. Her husband goes in the wagon just ahead of us. She was married the morning that she started for California. Not a very pleasant wedding tour. Camped in the sage brush.

Pioneers stand off an attack by Indians on the Oregon Trail.
Print from an old steel engraving.   Bert Webber collection

Thursday, August 14. Left our camp early to enter the canyon but it was farther than we supposed. Only got to the mouth of it by noon. Here we found some parts of wagons and yokes, chains [and goods] of emigrants that had probably been plundered last year. We found pieces of newspapers that had [articles] concerning the Civil War so it could not have been longer ago. After going up the canyon about four miles we came to a wagon that had been stopped. There was a new harness or parts of one, some collars and close by we saw the bodies of three dead men [on] the ground. They had been dead two or three weeks. Some one had been along and thrown a little earth over them but now they were mostly uncovered again. One had his head and face out, another his legs, a third his hands and arms. Oh! It was horrid to see. I wish all the Indians in Christendom were exterminated. We did not get through the canyon and were obliged to camp with the mountains on every side.

Friday, August 15. We were aroused this morning at one o'clock by the firing of guns and yelling of Indians answered by our men. The Captain calling "Come on you red devils." It did not take us long to [get] dressed. I hurried for the children and had them dressed and get into our wagon. I put up a mattress and some beds and quilts on the exposed side of the wagon to protect us. The firing was from the willows and from the mouth of the corral. There were two other trains with us. There are one hundred and eleven wagons of all and two hundred or more men. The firing did not continue long or do any harm. Our men shot a good many balls into the willows but I presume they were not effective. We sat and watched and waited till morning. We yoked the cattle and turned them out with a heavy guard and several guards to clear the bushes. [We] cooked our breakfast and started. There were ball holes through three wagon covers in the Thompson train. Two men felt the balls whiz past their faces. [There was] an arrow near the

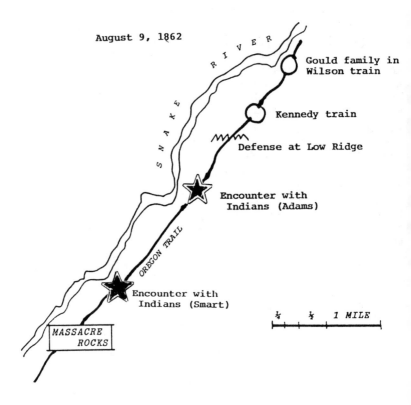

The site of the 1862 massacre along the Old
Oregon Trail in southern Idaho has been pre-
served as today's Massacre Rocks State Park.
Operated by the Idaho State Parks and Recreation Commission, the site is midway between
American Falls and the junction of Interstate
highways 80 and 86 east of Burley. Admission
is free.

mouth of the corral. We had gone only half-a-mile or so before we saw eight or ten [Indians] come out of their hiding places on ponies and go to our camping place to see, I suppose, if they had lamed or killed any men or cattle. The Captain had plenty of scouts out and an advance and rear and side guards. We nooned in a little valley but kept our eyes open to all that might be hidden in bushes and behind rocks. Camped by the side of a mountain. Near us on one side was a creek with willows along it. On the other a deep gulch [erroded] by rain. The Newburn and Thompson trains camped and [kept their] cattle with ours. The captains stationed picket guards in the ditch and on the sidehill. In the night we were all startled by the bark of the coyote which sounded very much like the Indians when they attacked us last night. The alarm gun was fired which awakened us all. After a while we concluded it was the [wild animals, not Indians] so we went back to bed. Most of the folks slept under their wagons, set up flour sacks and all manner of stuff [for protection]. We hung up a cotton mattress and some quilts and slept in the wagon. It is not an enviable situation to be placed in not to know at night when you go to bed whether you will all be alive in the morning. Came in sight of the "City of Rocks."

Saturday, August 16. Left our camp early, entered a canyon, followed it up between high hills or mountains among the rocks. It really has some of the appearance of a city at a distance. This has always been known as the worst place for Indian troubles on the Landers route. Some of the rocks are covered with names from 1852 up to the present year. I don't think there has been more than two trains through ahead of us. Did not stop for dinner. In the afternoon there came up a thunder shower real hard. We had to pitch the tent in the rain. It was quite a rarity. Was much pleasanter after it was over. It looked strange.

The clouds seemed to lie on the mountains. [That night] the men dug trenches and had picked guards.

Sunday, August 17. The weather was beautiful this morning. Traveled over very rough roads, that is up and down several steep hills. Came to Goose Creek this afternoon. Went up it two or three miles, were obliged to camp on it near willows and close by hills. Dug trenches again. Dug a deep hole on one of the hills for the pickets to stand in. Were not molested.

Monday, August 18. Left camp early. The weather was very warm but in the afternoon grew cooler, looked like rain, sprinkled some. We passed a chalk bed, likewise some very singular looking rocks on the right-hand side of the road. There were all sorts of shaped holes and men had written their names in and under them. Some of the men got soft stone and made some pipes. Some of them call the stone soap-stone. I don't know what it is. We followed up Goose Creek all day. The boys found some currants on the bank, some yellow, some black. Camped at night in the valley in some tall grass. Built entrenchments again, as the boys call it. I was startled again by the bark of the coyote but soon fell asleep again.

Tuesday, August 19. The road was very mountainous but not bad for mountain roads. About five o'clock we passed Rock Spring. Traveled five or six miles and camped in a valley in the tall grass. Did not get camped till after dark. Had to get supper by candle light. Let the tent stand tonight for the first time in a week on account the Captain thinking it would give a good chance for the Indians to [sneak] up behind it. [Jane Gould suggests here, we believe, the tents were merely tests for the Indians with the people sleeping in or under the wagons—the tents empty.] The Captain said we are now out of the Snake Nation for which I am truly grateful.

Wednesday, August 20. This morning was very cool.
We followed up a valley most of the forenoon with sage
brush in some places and tall grass in others. Nooned
on a kind of dead creek. Did not corral with the
other trains. Followed up a bottom some distance for
good grass, were obliged to camp in a very wet muddy
place with mosquitoes and sand wasps.

Thursday, August 21. The road was rough some of
the day. Some steep hills to pass over. We saw
several Indians today for the first time. They were
Snakes. One of them said he was chief. Three of the
men in the Newburn train burned the Indian's wigwams
[during the Indians] absence. The [Indians] came on
at noon and were very indignant about it and want pay
for [the damage]. Captain Walker told them who it was
who burned the [teepees]. The Indians got quite a
good deal of bread and bacon from different ones from
our camp. After being in trouble with them for so
long we are glad to let them be friendly if they will.
Albert, Lucy, and I went a short way from the road and
got our arms full of currant bushes laden with fruit,
both red and white. We ate what we wished and had
nearly two quarts to eat with sugar for supper. They
were very refreshing.

Friday, August 22. Arose this morning before sunrise. Was really cold. We are in sight of the Humboldt
Mountains. They are partly clothed in snow. Our roads
were hilly but good—quite dusty. We [had] been quite
free of [dust] for some time. Came over some steep
hills then down into a valley near a little grassy
creek where we nooned. Took the stove out and baked
some pancakes. Came most of the way in the afternoon
in the valley, crossed some small hills and camped
late near a small creek. [Still] have pickets out [in
case of Indian trouble].

Saturday, August 23. The Captain concluded to go
the mountain road down the Humboldt instead of the
bottom road as we found, to our sorrow this forenoon,

it was very rough and stony. It was very hard for
Mr. McMillin the man with consumption. He is getting
very weak. We found some nice choke cherries and
some service berries this forenoon. We did not
travel all day, only till noon. We have beautiful
water here. Oh dear, I do so want to get there. It
is now almost four months since we have slept in a
house. If I could only be set down with all the
folks at home I think there would be some talking as
well as resting. [My] Albert is so very miserable
[much of the time] that I don't enjoy myself as well
as I would if he was well. There have been Indians
around begging. We are glad to see them do so now
[instead of scouting and killing and stealing].

Sunday, August 24. After the first mile or two
today our road was not as rough as it was yesterday.
Had some bottom road. There were quite a number of
Indians came around this morning to pick up after us.
They would pick up the crusts and rinds and smell of
them then eat them just like a dog. Some of the
[Indian] children were in a state of nudity except a
rag around their shoulders under their arms. They
are Diggers. They picked up an old dish rag that I
had thrown away, put it in an old sack that they
carry. Nooned near a little creek close by the Newburn
and Thompson trains. Camped near a creek at sundown.
Did not get supper till after dark. Were visited
again by the Indians.

Monday, August 25. Did not start until late. We
had rough roads most of the time. Were visited again
this morning by the pests (Indians) again. Albert
found some nice black gooseberries as we were coming
along. Nooned by a beautiful little stream. Ellen
and I went down the creek a long way in pursuit of
berries but found none. The day is very warm indeed
but we are sure to have real cold nights and mornings.
Did not get into camp till after dark. Had wood and
water aplenty as there were three little creeks on

each side of us. I went to see Mr. McMillin. He is
not very well.

Tuesday, August 26. Had a very hard day's travel,
very dusty. Did not noon, camped very early on a nice
creek bottom.

Wednesday, August 27. The first thing I heard this
morning was that Mr. McMillin died at ten last night.
He died quite suddenly. Was buried early this morning.
They could not get boards to make a coffin. They dug
his grave vault fashion, made it just the right size
for him, high enough for him to lay in, then wider to
lay short boards over him. He was in his clothes with
a sheet around him. It seems hard to have to bury
one's friends in such a way. I do feel so sorry for
the poor wife and daughter [now] strangers in a strange
land. All of her relatives are in Ohio. We did not
stop at noon. Camped very late in the day in the
mountains. Had an excellent spring of water.

Thursday, August 28. Started early. Roads are
mountainous. Did not noon just kept going. Camped
on a creek, water very poor. Gus [who had been
traveling with us] left us tonight. He goes to help
Mrs. McMillin.

Friday, August 29. Started late. We could not
find our cow. I was afraid that the Indians had got
her but we found her near noon with the loose cattle.
[Our cow] had gone on with the Newburn train. Had
some of the worst mountain roads we have seen since
we left home. We came to where there had been Indian
depredations committed. There were feathers strewn
around, a broken wagon and a large grave with stones
over it. It had probably two or more persons in it.
There was a hat and nightcap found near, also some
small pieces of money. It had been done only a few
days. We camped after dark on the Humboldt River
[Nevada] for which we are very thankful.

[Saturday,] August 30. Did not start till noon [as] the cattle needed rest after so hard a day's work. Had somewhat a rough road about half the time. Camped early at a very pleasant place along the river.

[Sunday,] August 31. Had not gone more than a mile when we were stopped by a slough. There are several that got stuck in it. Some of us went back nearly to camp but got over well at last. Part of the road is stony and part real good. Nooned on the river. Camped after dark.

Monday, September 1. Had excellent roads most of the way. Did not stop for dinner. Camped on the river. There were Indians around. Nooned at a slough.

Tuesday, September 2. Traveled about twenty miles without feed or water. Camped on a slough.

Wednesday, September 3. After going two miles we came to a spring of water in the mountain side where we filled our cans. There has been a stone station there. Camped near noon for the rest of the day. There are numerous Indians around. They are Pah-Utahs, pronounced Pa-yoot. They are more intelligent than those we have seen heretofore. Alkali is plenty.

Thursday, September 4. Did not travel but half-a-day. I washed in the afternoon did not have time to dry them. Most of the vegetation here is sage and greasewood.

Friday, September 5. Had good roads, rather dusty, stopped early for dinner on the Humboldt. Here we are obliged to separate. Some of the train go the Honey Lake Route and some the Carson river route. We and 24 others go the latter. Our captain goes with the former. [Now] we seem like a family without a father. We think he is the best captain on the road. Some could hardly refrain from shedding tears. At parting, tears came into the captain's eyes as he bade goodbye. I never saw so much alkalie as there is in this river! In some places it is nearly an inch deep on the ground.

[The scene] looks as if there had been a light snow-fall. [We went] on [aways then] encamped on the river again. The captain and his men came also soon after as they could fine no ford across the river.

Saturday, September 6. Started this morning in our usual form excepting the few who are gone. The roads were real sandy. Two very hard hills to go up. Nooned by the river again. There the men [assembled] and elected a new captain. His name is Wood. I think he will be a good one [as] he and his wife have been through once before. He was captain [on his earlier] trip. There were [some] twenty or thirty Indians came in last night from Salmon River mines. They could most all speak English quite well. They live in Humboldt City. They way there is no gold in Salmon River mines.

Sunday, September 7. Did not start very early this morning. Most of the road is good, now and then a little sand. We travel most of the time near the river. Nooned early. We have heard that we have fifteen mile drive [ahead] without water or feed. Camped on the river. Had good grass. Some of the train had [fiddling and] a dance but we did not join them.

Monday, September 8. Started soom after sunrise this morning. Traveled four or five miles when we came to the fork in the road. One goes to Buena Vista and the other to Humboldt City. Captain Wood and all of the train except seven wagons, ourselves included with the seven, went to Buena Vista. After the fifteen mile drive without water or feed arrived within sight of Humboldt City. Here we found no grass. The cattle just had to browse willows. We here heard such discouraging accounts of our road to Carson River that the female portion of our [group] are almost discouraged. We sat by moonlight and discussed matters till near eleven o'clock. Had quite a number of gentlemen visitors during the evening. They say there

is no grass between here and Carson River—if not I
don't know what we can do.

Tuesday, September 9. When we arose the men told
us that if we were [to] hurry with our [chores] we
might have time to walk up and see the city so we
hurried. Lucy and I, Mrs. McMillin and Annie went.
We found it a long walk. I should think a mile all
of the way up hill. There are some two [dozen]
buildings, some of them rough stone and some adobe.
Some plastered and some no, mostly covered with cotton
cloth. We were called to see a woman who has a sick
husband. They are emigrants [and] have been here a
week. He has the typhoid fever [and they are] waiting
for him to recover. They want to cross Nevada mountains this fall. Provisions are high here. Flour is
$13.00 per cwt. Coffee 75 cts per pound. Sugar three
pounds for a dollar and bacon 35 cts per pound. Mrs.
McMillin and Annie went into a house and stayed a few
minutes. When she came out she said she intended to
[quit our train and] stay there. In the face of all
[our] opposition we [could not disuade her]. [In our
train we were short on provisions] I fear not enough
[to cross the mountains] so Gus was obliged to stay
too. I was sorry to leave him this side of California
as long as he started with us and is an old acquain-
tance. I was very sorry to leave Mrs. McMillin. It
does not seem like a good place for a woman to stay
[with] only four families here. The rest are single
men. We came on six or eight miles and stopped without much grass for noon. I am just as homesick as
I can be [and leaving Mrs. McMillin didn't help my
mind.] Her husband had died. I, with Gus, had been
looking after her ever since . I chanced to make
this remark and Albert has written it down. We had
a rough road all of the afternoon. Camped at what
is called Butcher's Canyon. There are three young men
here staying to recruit their teams. Took the cattle
up the mountains for feed.

Wednesday, September 10. Left our camp early. Had a rough road till near noon when we went down on what is called the river road. Traveled fifteen miles without water or grass. Camped at night in River Canyon. Had a good bunch of grass by driving the cattle up on the bluffs. Had Humboldt water to drink [right] out of the river. [The water] is not as bad as it was further up[stream].

Thursday, September 11. As the grass and water were good we thought it a good time to recruit our teams and stay a day. Ellen and I washed in the fore-noon and Lou in the afternoon. We made some pies and bread. We have no tea or coffee for over a week. We bought a little bacon, paid 35 cts per pound. The boys swam the river and got a large quantity of blue-berries. They grow on a large thorn bush. They are red and about the size of a large pea, are excellent for pies. In the evening we were very pleasantly astonished to see Mr. McMillin and Gus drive up. She found it would be too expensive living in the city through the winter so came on.

Friday, September 12. Started early this morning. Went three miles and came to a station close by the river. Went seven miles and came to another. Soon met three teams of freighters, they were taking [equipment for] a quartz mill to Star Canyon. Stopped for noon. Had good bunch grass but no water. [The] water was back two miles. Came on till we came to the alkali flats where the grass was poor and the men had to wade in near half-a-mile to get water for the stock. They only had half-a-pail full apiece.

Saturday, September 13. We left before sunrise and did not stop to get breakfast this morning. Had traveled two or three miles when Old Bill, our horse, gave out. He was so weak that he could not draw any longer. He is nothing but skin and bone. We unhar-nessed him and fed him a little flour and led him on till we came to a station. Mrs. McMillin let us have

one yoke long enough to draw one wagon to the station.
Here we got breakfast. Sold our small wagon for a
dressed sheep and a hundred pounds of hay, a large
price for a wagon. A man offered Albert 20 dollars
for Old Bill but we thought we could trade him for a
good pony so did not take it. Soon after leaving the
station we came on to the shore of Humboldt Lake,
followed it down till near sundown, when were obliged
to leave the horse. Left him some hay. Soon after
the rain began to fall, a very rare thing here. It
[stopped] raining [about] ten o'clock [just when we
finished setting up camp]. It was as dark as pitch.
[We were] at a station at the outlet of the lake.

Sunday, September 14. The sun shone as brightly
this morning as if it had never rained. Albert ate
his breakfast and went back for Old Bill. He went
seven miles and got [the horse] to within two miles
of the station [but] had to leave him. When he got
back he went to see the station keeper to see if [the
keeper] would give him anything for him. It took a
lot [of dealing]. At last he got an old saddle [on
trade] for the horse. Our one yoke of oxen now had
to draw all of the load which is very hard. Ellen
and Will Jones got a chance to go to Virginia City
free of charge for which we were very glad on account
of our heavy load. We are nearly out of provisions
too. We have to pay five cts. per lb. for hay.
Albert sold his whiffletrees and neck yoke for five-
and-a-half dollars. We had ten miles to go to get to
the desert. Got there at four o'clock crossed the
ferry, a kind of slough, which connects Carson and
Humboldt Lakes. The charge for crossing was 1.50.
We stopped to get supper and feed the stock and fill
our vessels with water. Albert went to the ferryman
to see if he could get a little coffee to make in the
night. He had none to sell but gave us nearly a
pound. We got started across the dreaded desert just
after sundown. The other four teams got their start
nearly an hour [ahead of us]. We traveled till one

o'clock then stopped and gave the teams some feed.
[We had lunch of] some bread, pie, and cold mutton
[after we] built a little campfire and warmed ourselves. Stayed only an hour and went on. Lou and I
walked a great deal. The roads are literally lined
with wagon irons and keg hoops and piles of bones
every few rods. Here and there a fresh corpse of a
once highly prized animal. The animals had hauled
thousands of pounds over a thousand miles then like
our good old horse Bill, just wore out.

Historical trail "leaver-ite" in Nevada's Forty-mile
Desert east of Carson City. Hasp and links of chain
from pioneer wagons. It's called "leaver-ite" because
it's OK to pick it up and look at it then *leave it right*
there for others to see.   Photo by Bert Webber

Monday, September 15. We came to the last ten
miles of the desert which is all bad sand just before
daylight. [We] stopped again and fed another cold
lunch. Boiled some coffee. Some of the stock would
not drink at all. The road is the worst I ever saw.
Lou and I walked the whole ten miles till we came to
within a mile of Ragtown. We saw the trees on Carson

River and thought we were most there but we kept going and going and it seemed as we never could get there. Charley was obliged to leave one of his cows only six miles from the ferry. She was not in the yoke. She was so weak she could not go any longer. We got to Ragtown about two o'clock in the afternoon. Our teams were nearly tired out. We went a mile above the town, which consisted of one house, and camped with the other four teams. We fed the teams some hay and stayed the night.

Tuesday, September 16. Arose early this morning and left. Went six miles farther up where there was good feed and had the pleasure of driving our wagons under some cottonwood trees which made a good shade. Mrs. McMillin and our two teams were all that spent the rest of the day here. Mr. Church lost another ox yesterday. [The] ox [had been] sick one day.

Wednesday, September 17. We started late this morning with the intention of [just] going six miles. Passed two stations and after going ten miles nooned, but on account of there being no feed we shall go six miles further. Had to go to the river [where] there is a station called Honey Lakes Smiths.

Thursday, September 18. Did not travel today. The boys worked for some hay. Lou washed. There is a large good looking house here. Mrs. McMillin went on this morning.

Friday, September 19. Had twenty-one miles to go today without grass. Traveled twelve miles to a well where we watered and fed some hay. Ate dinner ourselves. Were quite surprised to find Ellen here. She had hired out for a month for twenty dollars. Her husband is at Virginia City working for fifty dollars per month. After coming five miles farther we came to another well and a tent for a station. Found Mrs. McMillin here just ready to go. Went on together a mile-and-a-half. Lou and I and she and Annie walked so as to visit, at the end of the mile-and-a-half they turned off for the City and we went on to the river. We arrived there sometime after dark. Came along with the telegraph line once more. Very glad to see it once more.

Saturday, September 20. Met some people that we traveled with on the Platte River. They went Salt Lake route but both came here to this place the same day. When the men went for the stock they got three cows mired, one of them had to be dug out by oxen. [The cow] was so weak that she could not stand for some time but after a [while] she was [good enough] to be driven. Six miles up the river where we stopped at noon and stayed the next morning. Here at this ranch we found Dick Pritchard, one of our acquaintances from Mitchell County, Iowa. He has the ague. Sanford of the Wapain [*sic.*] was there too.

Sunday, September 21. The boys had some trouble about finding the cattle. Did not start till late. After going four miles we came to Dayton, a nice little village of one hundred or more houses. [NOTE: Dayton is on today's Highway 50 about 12 miles northeast of Carson City.] They have all been built since spring. They are of pine lumber which sells for 60 dollars per thousand. The town is very lively. There is a quartz mill in operation and it works on Sunday too. Fresh fruit sells here for 25 cts. per pound. [There are] apples, peaches, pears and grapes. Did not stop for dinner. There are houses and public wells all along on the road to Empire City which is ten miles from Dayton. We stayed at Empire all night. This town is not as large as Dayton but the streets are full of freight wagons. We see a great many fruit wagons here from California. There is quite a quartz mill here also. Money seems to be plenty, buildings going up fast, here is the place to make money especially for a man without a family. Can get fifty dollars and board per month for most any kind of work. Mechanics get more.

Monday, September 22. The men looked around some this morning so we did not get away very early. After going some five miles we saw Carson City off to the right, we only went to within three miles of there. There is a great deal of freighting going on from California over here. All kinds of provisions and groceries and fruits. Such large wagons as they use with six or eight mules or horses to a team carrying from three to six tons. I never saw horses and mules in better condition than those used for teaming. We bought some turnips today, paid five cts. per pound. They were very fine. Raised here. Saw some small patches of corn today. The corn is rather small. Camped at night at a ranch. Had to get our teams ranched—paid 12 1/2 cents per head [for their feed and care].

Tuesday, September 23. Had an early start but did not get along very fast for we stopped so much. Albert sold his harness and rifle at the town of Genoa for fifteen dollars cash. Charlie sold a good Colts revolver for six dollars. They bought some potatoes, the first we have had since the other side of Ft. Laramie, also some syrup and beef and bacon. Lou and I had to get some new shoes as ours were plain wore out. We got them here for about the same price we used to have to pay for them in the States. Passed by the Placerville toll road some time after noon to go on and take what is called the Big Tree route. There are three traveled roads through the mountains. The two I have just mentioned and what is called the Hennis Pass, which is farther north than the other two. We see some nice fields here. Camped near Fisher's store, tavern, and ranch. Hired the teams ranched [for the night].

Wednesday, September 24. Left camp early. Traveled seven miles before we entered the mouth of Carson Canyon. Nooned without feed, but rested and watered the cattle. Paid toll for a bridge and the Canyon road. The road is rather rough but not as

bad as some we have seen on the Landers Route through
the Bear River Mountains. Did not get camped till
sometime after dark. Stayed in Hope Valley. Hired
the teams to be ranched again, 20 cts. per head. The
ranchman told us there was seven inches of snow fell
here on the 21st of this month. Bought some nice
onions paid ten cts. per pound.

Thursday, September 25. Did not start early on
account of our late drive yesterday. We made some
elderberry pies. There are a great many of these
berries in the mountains. They are the sour ones
which make better pies than the sweet ones. The road
is very rocky. Nooned on Carson River. Ate our
dinner by the side of a large rock. Have met a
number of pack trains. They are very heavily laden.
It seems too bad for the poor creatures to have to
carry such great loads. They are driven by Greasors
[sic.] and Spaniards and Pay-ute Indians. Camped in
Faith Valley. Paid for ranching the cattle. Our
reason for coming this route was we thought there was
free feed [for the cattle but] have none [free] yet.

Friday, September 26. Left early this morning.
Had a good road for three or four miles. Came through
Charity Valley. There are some of the most beautiful
little valleys in those mountains [all] covered with
bright, fresh looking flowers. They're larkspur,
bluebell, honeysuckle and red flowers such as grow in
Iowa and Illinois. They look as if it is spring.
After traveling seven miles we crossed the summit.
It was a gradual ascent. At long last [we are] in
California! There are numerous little lakes surrounded with good grass. Nooned near one of them.
Our first dinner in California had tea, bread, milk
and pie. A pack train passed while we were eating.
Came to a ... [words missing]... river expecting to
find grass but it was fenced! It was near sundown
when we passed. Started up the hill which is four
miles long, went up nearly a mile, found a place that
we could drive out one side of the road and did so.

TO ALL PIONEERS WHO
PASSED THIS WAY TO WIN
AND HOLD THE WEST

ROUTE OF LANDER CUT-OFF.
FIRST GOVERNMENT FINANCED
ROAD IN WYOMING. OFFICIALLY
CALLED FT. KEARNEY, SOUTH PASS
AND HONEY LAKE ROAD. BUILT
IN 1858 FROM ROCKY RIDGE
TO FT. HALL TO PROVIDE SHORTER
ROUTE FOR EMIGRANTS.

ERECTED BY
WYOMING HISTORICAL LANDMARK COMMISSION
1947

Jane Gould mentions the "Landers Route" (page 77) and the "Honey Lake Route (page 68) when she describes the parting of the company on September 5. She is now in Nevada. The Lander Cut-off, (Lander Road) which usually comes to mind is in Wyoming. Photo by Bert Webber

Thought we would let the cattle pick what they could find. After turning them out the men went in search of grass and were very glad to find they could get the best of fresh green bunch grass.

Saturday, September 27. Had an early breakfast and started up the hill. We were willing to believe that it was four miles long by the time we got to the top. It is a mountain not a hill. Nooned without much feed. People living in the states have no idea how rough mountain roads can be. Camped in a small valley near a house that the roof was broken in last winter by snow. We had a splendid campfire in the evening. Sat up till late just talking by [our friendly fire.

Sunday, September 28. Had some trouble this morning about finding our cattle. Soon after starting had a very long steep hill to climb. The timber through here is fir and pine of two kinds, nut pine and white pine. About ten o'clock we came to a new road [which] is very well worked. The weather is very cold. We cannot ride all the time on account of it. We are somewhat afraid of a snow storm while we are here. We found some of the nicest large gooseberries I ever saw. They are prickly. We nooned on the side of the road in the timber, built a large campfire but that did not keep us warm on both sides. Did not camp till near sundown. Camped in a pine forest, a very dusty place. Saw a very little oak today for the first time since we left Iowa. It grows gnarly.

Monday, September 29. 'Twas very cool this morning when we started. There was ice in the [coffee] pot. The boys think it quite a hardship to ride the horse in this weather. Came through the most beautiful timber I ever saw. Passed the large tree called the Mother of the Forest. It is 78 feet in circumference and 360 ft. high. There is a staging built around it up 160 feet from the ground, there are names cut in the wood all over it. It is redwood. I thought it was as large as a tree could be but I found soon after that there was one still larger. After going a half-a-mile we came to the famous Big Tree Hotel. It is a large three story frame house, richly furnished and well kept, so I am informed. After getting our early supper we went to inspect the grove of world renouned large trees. We went through the grove, saw the "Three Sisters." One has been killed by fire. The "Pride of the Forest," the "Pioneers Cabin," the "Miners Cabin," "Uncle Tom's Cabin," "George Washington," and a great many other large trees with names. The name is on a tiny placard nailed on the tree, the height and size of the tree. I don't believe this grove had its equal in the world. There are several swings in the grove [so] Lou and I had a little swing [ing]. At last we went to see the Big Tree. It has been cut down. It took two men 27 days It is bored with augers. It is 29 feet in diameter. On the stump is a ballroom [dance] floor. It is sixteen sided wound sic top and green blinds for door and windows. It is plenty large enough for one set to dance. The top of the stump is smoothed so there is no floor but that except where it is filled around the outside. Lou and I danced the schottische on it. The bottom part of the log is near. There is a ladder 30 feet long to climb up on it. We went on to it. It is covered with names. There is a bowling alley on the remainder of the tree as it lays. We were all through it. Mr. Graham, the owner of the premises, has from forty to sixty boarders all through the summer who come here to rusticate, besides having visitors from all parts of America and some from Europe to see the wonderful forest. The scenery is beautiful. There are some ladies there now from Stockton and Sonora, also some from the other cities of California. There are saddle horses and carriages and horses kept here for the use of visitors. We met today a gentleman after his children over to Carson City. We have some information about them. They came through in our train after the Indian robbery, were among the robbed. He was very much pleased to hear from them and to show his gratitude gave us some two dozen pears and apples. The first California fruit we had eaten. [NOTE: According to the American Guide Series book *California; A Guide to the Golden State,* see reading list at end of book, there is a description of the area Jane Gould describes (page 493) identifying the great forest as Calavaras Big Tree Grove. The hotel Jane Gould describes may have been The Mitchler Hotel which was built in 1856. The town of Murphys, which she mentions in her entry for September 30, is also identified in this guide. The town is still operating and has postal ZIP of 95247. The town is on Highway 4.]

Tuesday, September 30. The forest is beautiful this forenoon. The country hilly. We passed several ranches, arrived near night at Murphy's, a village of 200 or more houses. It is a mining town. There is a good deal of business done here. There is considerable fruit growing. Some of it has been gathered. They raise apples, peaches, pears, and grapes. Albert bought some grapes and apples. I prefer the grapes to all others. Grapes are six cts. per pound. Charley got some sweet potatoes. They are four cts. per pound. We also had some peaches but they were not ripe and were not very good but very large. We saw some live oak today.

Wednesday, October 1. Our roads are rather rough. I walked on before the teams two miles or more, called at a farm for a drink and to rest. Had the pleasure of sitting in a large rocking chair, the first time for five months. They had plenty of fruit trees. Albert called for me and bought some fine grapes and a pail of tomatoes. The lady of the house gave me some roses and verbenias. They were beautiful and fragrant. Nooned on a hill. Had bunch grass for the teams. I have a sore nose today by way of variety. We came by a distillery and in sight of a little town by the name of Altaville. [NOTE: Altaville is at junction of California State Highways 49 and 4 at 1,525-feet altitude, one mile from Angel's Camp and about fifty miles east of Stockton.] Have passed through a good deal of old mining ground. The country is not settled much. We are in the foothills yet. The grass and weeds are perfectly dry. It looks strange to see the face of the earth so dry and the trees all so green, just as green as they were in spring. Camped in some oak openings, ranched our cattle. All the water they use here comes from the mountains brought in spouts.

Thursday, October 2. The roads are hilly yet. I never saw so dry looking a country. Most of the buildings we have seen today are little miner's huts. The country is all dug over and cut up with sluices. Did not stop for dinner. Passed a reservoir to keep water for the purpose gold mining. Camped opposite a hotel under some fine oak shade trees. Two of the little girls came to see us in the evening. They told us we would be out of the hills in two miles more travel.

Friday, October 3. Left our encampment early. After a few miles we came to more level country but so dry and uncultivated. Nooned by a creek near a house. Bought hay. Had twelve miles to go without food or water for the cattle. There was one old house but it was vacant. Arrived at the first house in the settlement of the San Joaquin Valley. On this road at ten o'clock at night the moon shone brightly. We pitched our tent and got supper. In this part of the country all of the water is pumped by the power of windmills. The orchards are not as they are in the states. [NOTE: Jane Gould probably did not know that California had become a state twelve years earlier— September 9, 1850, and plausibly used the word "states" for lack of a better description.] They are so small and the trees so close together. Every garden has its windmill to irrigate it. Saw today Mount Diablo [3,849 feet altitude] the highest mountain in California. It is in the coast range. [NOTE The highest mountain in California is Mt. Whitney at

14,494 feet altitude but Jane must be forgiven as she was new to the state, still just "passing through" and would not have known of much other than what she saw.]

Saturday, October 4. We're within twelve miles of Stockton this morning. Thought we could only go to town and see if we could find a place to settle ourselves in for the winter. Came into a farming country, very large ranches and good houses. They raise grain without irrigation forty and fifty bushels to the acre. Charlie and Albert are looking for situations today. Called at a large house where there was an orchard. Bought us a treat of fruit: apples, peaches, pears, figs and grapes. The peaches were 5 cts. per pound, the grapes 6, the apples 8, pears 10, the figs 12½. Figs are a very sweet rich fruit, two or three are as many as one cares to eat, although they are small. It began raining about two o'clock. We camped in a field opposite a fine house. At three o'clock the master of the house told us to come and get all of the tomatoes we could use. It was quite a treat to us. We went to get a pail of potatoes. He also gave those to us. Rained till dark then cleared off.] The house cost fourteen thousand dollars the owner said].

Sunday, October 5. Stayed here in the same place for the purpose of looking around and resting the teams and ourselves. Are within two miles of town. Borrowed some papers at the house to read. After we had gone to bed we heard the alarm bell ring, looked out and saw a large bright fire. It was in town. The firemen came but were too late. The house burned to the ground.

Monday, October 6. Lou washed today. The men went to town [Stockton] to see what was to be seen and done. Albert came home [to our wagon] sick. He went to bed and did not sit up for a few minutes the rest of the day. [When in town, the men] found no place that suited them. Mrs. Burkett, the lady of the house [near where we had camped], called to see us, was quite pleasant. She and her husband also called in the evening. There was raised forty bushels to the acre of volunteer wheat on this place last year. That is where the wheat of last year came up from, what was wasted while harvesting. The water was so high here in this field that the ground could not be ploughed or sewed but still they got a good crop of wheat. They don't plant tomatoes but once, they selfsow. The garden and young fruit trees and flowers here look like early spring, just as fresh. The hay that is made is oat hay, cut while the oat is green. We see no other kind. It is a very common thing to raise a good crop of hay on an oat field of the last year, what they call a volunteer crop. I never saw as nice wheat as we see here, and beautiful fine flour. Hiram is at work chopping wood, gets one dollar per day and his board. Times are said to be very dull here. It seems so to us.

Tuesday, October 7. Are still staying here. Albert seems to be no better. I almost have the "blues" having to camp out and Albert sick too. While speaking of figs I forgot to say that they bear all of the time from June till November. This day seems long. I can't sit myself to sewing although I have so much to do. I believe I am melancholy.

Wednesday, October 8. Arose this morning with the intention of going to town. Lou and I went over a few minutes to call on Mrs. Burkett. She had a visitor from town. She regaled us with some very fine peaches. Went to town and pitched our tent. A lady called by the fence and told us of a house to rent, also gave us some green corn, the first we have seen this year. Charlie went with her to the house [and] made a bargain provided it pleased all around which it did. We picked up and went right over. Slept in a house the first time for over five months. The house is one block east of the Lunatic Asylum. The block which intervenes is vacant. We are to board the

owner of the house, Mr. Bray. The house is quite
convenient. We will pay ten dollars per month rent.
The house is over half-a-mile from the business part
of town.

Farewell to the old
journal.

JANE A. GOULD

EPILOGUE

Jane Gould quit her diary on the day they rented a house in Stockton, California. How long they were there isn't known, but they next appear in the Santa Clara County town of Lexington. Albert's health seems to have temporarily improved so he took a job as a millwright in McMillan's Sawmill a few miles south of the village of Los Gatos. Apparently he died in this area for his widow then was hired as a cook for the same firm apparently in a logging camp or at the mill.

A bull-team driver who worked at the logging camp, one Levi Tourtillott, met Jane at the camp presumably in the dining room. They married February 20, 1864. Levi obtained a ranch through the Homestead Act about fifteen miles east of San Jose in the foothills of the Diablo Range of mountains. Their existence on the ranch was apparently hand-to-mouth but they made every effort to stick it out.

They were confronted by the City of San Jose which claimed the land due to an old Spanish law under the Pueblo Land Act. The City demanded Levi pay $5.00 per acre for each of the 320 acres which he did. Then along comes General Henry Morris Naglee, a West Pointer retired from the U. S. Army with an 1857 patent on the land issued under settlement of claims between Spain and the United States following the Mexican War. The property seems to have been a part of Rancho Los Coches ("The pigs") and was so named because in Mission San Jose days the area was the mission's swine acreage. Naglee had been promised land by the U. S. Government, in exchange for his

86

willingness to take troops from New York to fight in the Mexican War. Data on the General is from *Historic Spots in California* included in the reading list. Levi and Jane Tourtillott paid him off too, for an undisclosed price, and kept the ranch.

In the meantime, Jane had responded to her wifely responsibilities and presented Levi with five children which made seven children her total. As a result of Levi's exposure to the elements while working in the forests as a logger, he was apparently suffering rhumatoid arthritis. The condition we find listed at the time was just "inflammatory rhumatism" a pretty general term. Not able to work the ranch, he leased it and moved into San Jose with his wife and family. He died in 1876. Jane had now lost two husbands. Her two earlier boys had grown and left home so she took her four younger sons and daughter to live with her married son, George Gould, at his place in the mountains east of Morgan Hill.

Following the expiration of the lease on the ranch, she went back there with her family until 1896 when she and her daughter, Millie Augusta, who was an artist and unmarried, moved back into San Jose. In the meantime her four Tourtillott sons had grown and moved away. Millie died in 1911. Jane died in 1917 at age 84 years.

Of her earlier family, George moved to western Oregon, somewhere in Douglas County then to Coos County. He died in 1921. He had four children, three sons and a daughter.

The younger son, Frank, became a lawyer and practiced in San Francisco. One report suggests he spent two terms in the state legislature. He died in 1918. He had two sons and one daughter.

On the Tourtillott side, in order, was son Howard, a machinist. Died 1936 at Lindsay. He had one son and two daughters.

Son Ernest, also of Lindsay, was a farmer and died in 1927. He also had one son and two daughters.

Their daughter, Millie, mentioned earlier, died in the San Jose residence in 1911. Unmarried.

Son Walter became a physician in Porterville. He died at age 78. He had three daughters.

Son True T. Tourtillott worked for the California State Hospital (plausibly the Agnews Branch near San Jose) and lived to 80 years. Apparently he had only one son, True Sherburne Tourtillott. He was principal in Quincy Elementary School 1949-1951 school years. The editor attempted to reach him but learned from the California State Teachers Retirement System in Sacramento that he died in in 1965. ☐

A TRIBUTE

There is reason to believe the transcriber of the
original Jane Gould diary was her son True T.
Tourtillott. We have a short, emotional piece,
plausibly from her eulogy, this tribute known to
have been written by him:

> During all these years of privation
> we never knew our mother to show the
> slightest degree of defeatism or lack
> of faith that, no matter what problems
> confronted us, all would be well in the
> end. There were many, many occasions
> when a weaker heart or one with less
> faith in the wisdom of the Creator
> might have given up in despair. Always
> calm and always cheerful, she radiated
> sunshine and courage to those with whom
> she came in contact, and her high sense
> of truth and justice commanded the
> respect and admiration of all right-
> thinking people.
>
> A neighbor once remarked when she
> observed mother driving a team of
> horses on a return trip from the vil-
> lage with her flock of five youngsters
> huddled about her in the old spring
> wagon, "There goes the Queen of Mothers."
>
> And that's just what she was, God
> bless her.
>
> T. T. TOURTILLOTT.

BIBLIOGRAPHY

Early Idaho Atlas. [Historical Atlas Series] Binford & Mort. (1978)

Ellison, Robert S. *Independence Rock*. Ye Galleon (1985)

Franzwa, Gregory M. *Maps of the Oregon Trail*. The Patrice Press. (1982)

_____ *The Oregon Trail Revisited*. The Patrice Press. (3rd Ed. 1983)

Haines, Aubrey, L. *Historic Sites Along the Oregon Trail*. The Patrice Press. (2nd Ed. 1985)

Hansen, Harvey, (Ed.) *California; A Guide to the Golden State*. [American Guide Series] Hastings House. (Rev. Ed. 1967)

Hoover, Mildred B. *Historic Spots in California*. Rev. 3rd Ed. by Wm. N. Abeloe. Stanford Univ. Press. (1965)

Mattes, Merrill J. *The Great Platte River Road*. Nebraska State Historical Society. (1969)

Moeller. Bill & Jan. *The Oregon Trail, A Photographic Journey*. Beautiful America. (1985)

Paden, Irene D. *The Wake of the Prairie Schooner*. The Patrice Press. (1985)

Webber, Bert. *The Oregon & Applegate Trails Diary of Welbor Beeson in 1853*. Webb Research Group. (1987)

For the complete list of 14 different books about the Oregon Trail published by Webb Research Group, send self-addressed stamped envelope to the publisher at address in front of this book.   Thank you.

INDEX

Numbers in *italic* are photographs

Of several published authors in Oregon-California Trails
Association, here are Aubrey Haines, Bert Webber, Merrill
Mattes, Gregory Franzwa. See the bibliography for some of
their books. Photo made at Fort Churchill in Nevada during an OCTA field trip into the Forty Mile Desert.

Rediscover History   Help Save the Trails

In 1982 a group of dedicated trail enthusiasts and sc
olars founded the Oregon-California Trails Associatic
to help save the trails. It has interceded many time
to help planners route their roads and pipelines away
from historic trails. But that is a big job and a cos
ly one. OCTA needs help. Join OCTA and receive the
handsome quarterly *Overland Journal*. Annual convent·
are held in major trail cities highlighted by low cos
field trips, scholarly presentations and slide shows
where everybody has a lot of fun rediscovering histor

For membership application, write to The Oregon-
California Trails Association, National Headquarters,
P. O. Box 1019 , Independence, MO 63104